CROSSBOWS

CROSSBOWS

FRANK BILSON

HIPPOCRENE BOOKS
New York

Dedicated to my nephew Kenneth Nunn in recognition of
his encouragement and help

Hippocrene Books
171 Madison Avenue
New York, N.Y. 10016

New Edition 1983

Library of Congress Catalog Card Number 74-16694
ISBN 0-88254-701-1

Manufactured in the United States of America

Contents

5

List of Illustrations

7

LIST OF ILLUSTRATIONS

IN TEXT

*Figs 1, 2, 3, 4, 6, 7, 8, 9, 10 and 19 were redrawn from illustrations
in Sir Ralph Payne-Gallway's* The Crossbow *(first published 1906)*

8

Introduction: Why the Crossbow?

The inborn urge to handle a weapon and shoot something, presumably passed down from the time when our forefathers did not eat if they could not successfully hunt, these days finds very little fulfilment with most of us. Not only is there the prohibitive cost of grouse moors but there is the pressing need for conservation and the general discouragement of the use of firearms by virtually every known authority. Fortunately an increasing number of people are finding an answer to this urge in using some of the oldest types of weapons for competitive target shooting of one sort or another.

There is another inherent urge in most of us; the urge to make or do something useful. This is particularly true of those who are tied to a desk most of the day and therefore have little opportunity to use their hands creatively. Obviously with working hours getting shorter there is a greater need and at the same time better opportunities to fulfil these inherent urges. Making one's own weapons and shooting them in competition with other members of a club has not only proved to be possible but is one of the most satisfying ways of enjoying open-air sport.

In England and Scotland a few people became interested in making and shooting crossbows round about the early 1960s, and a firm that had been one of the first to make composite handbows in England and had been selling them for some years began marketing a modern crossbow. This effort was encouraged by a request from Dr Short of the Cambridge University

9

Veterinary College to supply crossbows with hypodermic darts suitable for tranquillising animals both wild and domestic. These crossbows are now being used by zoos and game reserves in many countries.

In 1964, with the encouragement of several archers such as Jack Flinton of Scarborough and Eric Baldwin of Essex, the British Crossbow Society was formed. Stanley Turner of Chesterfield and Terry Stewart of Scotland have also helped to spread the interest in the sport.

In North America there are growing opportunities for crossbowmen to shoot in handbow tournaments on separate targets provided for them. Also more and more crossbows are being used in field shooting (see page 54).

Many archers who have enjoyed the challenge and thrill of hitting the middle of the target with modern composite longbows are finding that similar thrills can be experienced when they use the beautiful modern crossbows. It is true that the mechanics involved mean that less strain is put on the muscles, while a similar degree of accuracy is more easily attained. But at least the sport offers an opportunity to get away from the plague of 'target shyness' for a time and yet still enjoy an open-air sport and the company and joy of competing against kindred spirits. In other words, a bow is a bow and it can provide interest, pleasure and exercise for a sportsman, when it is released by the fingers, with or without the help of a trigger.

CROSSBOWS

CHAPTER 1

The Construction of the Crossbow

The overriding points to be striven for in good weapon design are, first, balance, which can be achieved only by trial and error, second, an apparent simplicity of line, which means ridding the surface of every irregular knob, joint, lever and unsightly angle, and third, accuracy in shooting, which can be affected by the kind of stock used, the groove the missile runs in, the angle at which the prod is attached to the stock, and the size, weight and fletching of the bolts.

STOCK DESIGN

Looking at a well-designed crossbow some may imagine that the stock is a very simple unit to design and that in order to be a good weapon a crossbow needs only some means of holding the prod at the front and, farther back, a method of releasing the string with a trigger. This is far from the truth, for there are several complicated factors to be considered.

Perhaps most important of all is the need for a perfectly straight groove along which the missile will run. Any curve or irregularity in this groove will cause inaccuracy because the bolt or dart will be travelling at up to 200mph (320km/h) and will therefore hit any curve with great force. Friction will reduce the range of the bolt, so in addition to being straight, the groove must also be smooth and polished. The depth and width of the groove will govern the type of bolt and the height of the fletching to be used (see page 66).

11

If the stock is made of wood, the best way of ensuring that it stays straight is to make it of three or five thick laminations from stable hardwood glued together in such a way that the grain of the two outer laminations runs horizontally while the grain of the next lamination runs vertically. As there is a certain amount of springiness in steel and aluminium alloy it is no use expecting separate grooves made of these metals to prevent any twist in stocks made of a single piece of wood. It is essential to start with a good foundation for the weapon by using only well-seasoned and laminated wood.

The shape of the butt also needs careful consideration. Some people hold the mistaken idea that the crossbow butt should be the same shape as a rifle butt. This is quite wrong. The velocity of a rifle bullet is such that very little difference in elevation is needed between 50yd and 100yd (46m and 92m). With a crossbow, however, a much higher trajectory is needed at 100yd, so you must be able to slide the butt much farther down the shoulder so as to achieve the required elevation when aiming at the longer distance. This means that the crossbow butt must have quite a long and shallow curve compared to the short, deep curve of the rifle butt.

Another important consideration is how to prevent yourself damaging your fingers by allowing them to get in the way of the string when shooting. It is all very well to maintain that you should have been trained to keep them out of the way. Nine times out of ten you may be able to do so. But there comes the tenth time when, because you are concentrating on the centre of the target or in the excitement of the chase, all else is forgotten until you suddenly feel as if the tops of your fingers have been carried away with the bolt. To insure against such an accident it is wise to make the stock at least 3⅞in (10cm) deep at the point where the supporting hand will be grasping it. This, and long deep grooves in which the tips of the fingers can get a grip, will considerably reduce the likelihood of any such accident. Some crossbow designers seem to prefer the pistol grip, similar to that fitted to a Thompson sub-machine gun, but this does not entirely prevent danger to the fingers because the stock can still be held other than with the pistol grip, with the fingertips above the stock.

Provision for front and back open sights must be made, or a dovetail mounting for a telescope sight provided. For target shooting a good telescopic sight is preferable, but for hunting and tranquillising animals adjustable open sights are best because they give a view of the whole animal and the particular part to be hit can therefore be clearly seen.

Various triggers and catches have been designed and used down the ages (see page 37). Some are quite complicated but none the less effective. The modern tendency, however, is to use a strong but simple mechanism. For the sake of safety some form of guard must be fitted round the trigger so that it cannot be released by mistake. This can be provided in the design of the stock or alternatively a separate metal guard can be screwed on.

Up to 80lb (37kg) or 90lb (42kg) pull on the prod can be dealt with by hand, but even then it is a help to have a stirrup against which to pull the string when cocking. For a pull of over 100lb (46kg) it is essential to provide a lever of some sort for cocking the string (see page 28).

PRODS

The materials used in making the 'bow' part of crossbows have varied in different countries and at different periods of history, though it is true to say that in general the materials used and the method of constructing the archery bow of the period were also used to construct the crossbow prod. There is one notable exception to this, however. It appears that while the English longbow, preferably made of yew, was still the choice of archers in Europe, crossbow makers changed to steel for their prods as soon as that metal became available in the eighteenth century, in spite of the considerable danger when the metal fatigued and broke.

In China and the Far East, where crossbows appear to have been first made, bamboo would have been the most natural material for the prod. We have plenty of evidence that this was indeed used. Yet it is difficult to avoid the assumption that when composite bows, constructed of horn, wood and sinew, became the paramount weapon in the East these materials were used for the construction of crossbow prods as well. Although it was an expensive method of construction, requiring a considerable time for shaping the various parts and for the glue and the finish to mature, the vastly increased speed and range would have made this construction vital for crossbows used in war.

Crossbow composite prods were of course shorter than the normal archery bow but were constructed in a similar way, though without the extreme curves in the two limbs of Asiatic handbows. The centre core of the wood lamination was thicker in the middle and tapered evenly to the nocks at each end. On the forward surface of this wood were glued layer after layer of animal sinew. If the tendon is cut from the heel of a large animal such as a bullock or cow and soaked in water with lime for a considerable period it can be beaten out and pulled apart into silky shreds. These can then be covered with hot fish glue or isinglass and built up in layers on the wood. As the sinew dries it shrinks and can take a tremendous tensile strain.

On the other side of the wood core were glued flat strips of buffalo horn, which were able to withstand great compressive stresses. These two opposing materials therefore allowed a crossbow prod to be made comparatively short without any fear of its breaking; being short, the limbs would recover extremely fast, driving the bolt forward with great speed.

A few years ago aluminium alloy prods were tried in place of the heavier steel. It was thought that the lighter metal would recoil faster for the same weight of pull. This was undoubtedly true, but as with any type of metal under stress, constant bending eventually caused the limbs to crystallise and shatter, with dangerous results. Metal should never be used for crossbow prods unless it is bound with strong self-adhesive tape to prevent jagged pieces flying about if a break should occur.

Solid fibreglass prods are a better proposition because they seldom break. By solid fibreglass I mean fibreglass-reinforced plastic. Just as with reinforced concrete long iron rods are embedded in the mixture before it sets, giving it a very much greater strength, so fibreglass threads are embedded in liquid resin so that when it sets solid its strength is very much greater. Although the result is a very strong and resilient material it still has one disadvantage: it is certainly much lighter than steel, but neither the glass nor the resin can really be called light in weight, and this combined weight tends to slow down the recovery of the bow and, of course, the speed of the bolt.

The Asiatic composite-construction bows worked on what is known in mechanics as the stress skin principle. This means that the outer surfaces of both the back and front of the bow do the bulk of the work and the inside 'core' needs only to be a strong but light material—the lighter the better. Light wood is the obvious choice. The composite bow or prod with a thin fibreglass sheet on both sides and with light maple wood laminations for the core easily outstrips in speed any other material at present available.

I have been experimenting with carbon fibre sheet but so far satisfactory gluing has been a problem.

METHODS OF ANCHORING THE PROD

Fixing the prod to the stock is not as straightforward as it may at first appear. To minimise friction the ideal would be to have the bolt shooting through the centre of the prod. But this would weaken the centre of the prod far too much and also make it very difficult to fix properly into the stock. The prod must therefore be fixed below the top level of the stock and at such an angle that when the string is undrawn it does not bear so hard on the stock that it causes friction or, when fully drawn, stand so high above the bolt groove that it would lift the bolt out while it was driving it forward. A compromise has to be employed and this has led to a variety of methods being used at different times.

The earliest method, as far as we know, was employed by the crossbow makers of the Chinese Han period. The front of their stocks was so shaped that it accepted the middle of the prod. Farther back along the stock a hole was cut completely through from side to side, enabling the prod to be bound to the stock with thongs of sinew. The advantage of sinew for this purpose is that when it is soaked in water it becomes soft and elastic and can easily be used for binding under tension. When it dries it shrinks and makes the binding extremely secure. This method of fixing meant of course that the centre of the prod was below the channel along which the bolt ran. To lessen the friction of the string on the sides of this channel the prod was set at a slight angle, so that when it was fully drawn the ends of the limbs came above the level of the channel.

For many centuries and in many countries this method of lashing the prod to the front of the stock was employed. Following that, and possibly to overcome the problem of the prod becoming loose whenever the sinew binding became wet, crossbowyers began fixing the prod in a hole cut *through* the stock. It was secured with a half-round wedge and bound with normal twine through a hole cut farther back in the stock (page 58).

When more metal was used in the construction of crossbows, including steel prods, metal side plates began to be used. These were called bow-irons and were fixed on to the side of the stock. Metal wedges and adjusting screws made it possible to secure various thicknesses of steel prods according to the strength needed. In some cases stirrups to aid cocking were made in one piece with the bow-irons.

Some of the cheaper crossbows merely had the steel prods screwed into the front end of the stock (see page 58). This may have been sufficient for a weak prod but it seems likely that the screw holes were a source of danger.

Page 17
Crossbow
shooting
with
retrievable
targets at
a sports
exhibition
in London

Page 18
Eric Baldwin,
President of
Essex CAA,
clout shoot-
ing at 180yd

The more modern method of securing the prod is to cut a slot upwards from the underpart of the stock, taking care not to weaken the stock by cutting into the bolt channel. The prod is then slid up into this slot with the protection of suitable leather or felt padding and locked in place with a cap screwed up. This method is particularly suitable for fixing the modern composite prod, in which the fibreglass must not rub against any hard surface.

The angle at which the prod is fitted to the stock must be a compromise between the vertical and 10° but the exact angle between those two must be carefully worked out according to the length of draw. In a crossbow having a draw-length of about 14in (35cm) the prod must be fitted into a slot cut about 5° from the perpendicular. To lessen the possibility of the string rubbing hard on top of the stock and checking its speed some prods are shaped with the top edge level but the bottom edges of the limbs tapered upwards as illustrated (see Fig 12).

For flight shooting, where freedom from any friction is so important, prods are often fitted over the top of the stock in steel brackets and a section of the centre of the prod cut away to allow free passage for the bolt.

BOLTS AND QUARRELLS

The age-old controversy among all who shoot projectiles certainly involved crossbowmen to a great extent. For greater penetration some would choose a heavy bolt, relying upon its sheer weight to carry it through any shield or plate armour, while others argued that the superior speed of the lighter bolt would carry it just as far in penetration and need a less powerful prod.

So down the ages there have been many different shapes of heads, different lengths of shaft and various overall weights in crossbow bolts. It is quite likely that some of the metal points found in the ground and classed as arrow-heads are in fact bolt-heads with the wooden shaft rotted away. There is no doubt that in any period of history the construction of crossbow bolts followed very closely the general construction of the longer arrow for the handbow. The purpose for which they were used governed to a great extent the shape of the head with which they were fitted.

When chain mail armour was the best protection available the bodkin point was extensively used. This iron or steel head was very long and narrow, with a square or sometimes diamond shape in the section. The long, narrow point was calculated to find its way through and open up the links in the chain mail. The armourers' eventual answer to this type of bolt was plate armour with cleverly placed angles, so that from most directions the bolt could only give a glancing shot that would not pierce the plate. Although this type of armour was heavier and more difficult to fight in, it became almost universal with mounted knights, indeed with their horses too, because it gave greatly improved protection from arrows and crossbow bolts. However, arrowsmiths and bolt makers eventually found an answer even to this plate armour. They developed a square type of steel head with four sharp corners, so placed that at least one of them caught in the armour and delivered a blow that, from a strong bow, could unhorse a man, or at least severely dent if not pierce the plate. These bolts were called 'quarrells' and were widely used against armoured knights. The wounds these quarrells inflicted, especially on those without adequate armour, were terrible. If an archer or crossbowman 'picked' a quarrell to use against anyone he was truly out to kill.

In the hunting field and against enemies without armour the better-known broadhead bolt was more commonly used. Originally made of bronze and later of steel, these heads were forged into two wide blades sometimes totalling 1in (2·5cm) width. The edges and point could of course be very sharp and the penetration was deadly. These broadheads inflicted a clean wound and killed by haemorrhage, whereas the quarrells inflicted a terrible lacerated wound and killed by shock, which is alleged to be much more painful.

An authentic case of two bowmen hunting deer in America has been recorded. They had seen a buck and foolishly decided that one of them should go round the far side of it while the second should follow it from the near side. The one on the near side saw some movement in a bush and took a shot, presuming it was the buck. Unfortunately it was his colleague! After months in hospital the luckless bowman recovered and wrote down his experiences. He explained that he did not realise that he had been hit until he saw the arrow sticking out of his side and then promptly fainted. Presumably the reason for this is that the blade was so sharp and travelling at such high speed that there was little immediate shock and pain, even though flesh and arteries had been cut through.

No doubt it was the terrible wounds caused by the quarrells that caused successive popes to rule against the use of crossbows in war between Christian countries. (They held that their use against infidels was justified, however.)

For shooting birds a bolt with a wide crescent head, sometimes modified to a wide V shape, was used. These heads were sometimes as much as approx 2½in (7cm) wide, with the inside edge of the crescent sharpened to a cutting edge. Presumably the idea was that the extreme width of the blade had more chance of hitting the quarry than the narrow blade of a bodkin head, for instance. Against this advantage must be put the fact that in my experience these wide flat blades tend to 'sail' or veer off to one side in flight. Even the more moderate two-bladed broadhead bolt, with the head very carefully fitted straight in line with the shaft, has a tendency to sail off course when losing speed. For this reason by far the best hunting head for big game, that is anything from a coypu to an elephant, is the three-bladed version of the broadhead. The blades can be narrower and still be equally effective; as they are placed at equal distances around the shaft there is no tendency for them to veer off. They shoot

21

straight and have great penetrating power. The three blades are placed in line with the three feathers so that one blade and one feather fit down the groove in the stock. It was thought that this was a modern invention until it was discovered that it was used centuries ago in the Balkans. Some even claim they are mentioned by Homer.

For rough shooting, when trees and stumps may be the targets, a field blunt is a better bolt to use. Instead of a sharply tapered point as for target shooting this has a small 'post' at the front, followed by a shoulder which is the full diameter of the shaft. The 'post' enters the tree or ground and the wide shoulder prevents the bolt from entering too far, so that it can be recovered.

For modern target shooting in which three or six bolts are shot there is nothing to beat the tubular aluminium alloy bolt. This can be matched very exactly in weight and length and fitted with identical piles. The only possible variation is the fletching. Even then if extruded plastic vanes are glued on with a good fletching jig, there should be no variation between one bolt and another.

In actual shooting, however, it can be demonstrated that of, say, twelve matched bolts six will habitually group on the target more tightly than the other six. The use of these tighter grouping six in a major tournament can help a serious competitor to achieve much higher scores. The point is that each bolt is shot several times in a round, so if one does not group with the others because of some slight defect it will lose two or four points every time it is shot. However carefully made, bolts with wooden shafts can never be so closely matched as those with the modern aluminium alloy tubing shafts. They are, of course, much cheaper and easier to make and are therefore ideal for non-serious target practice, small vermin hunting and so on.

In competitive target shooting the most important equipment therefore is a first-class set of carefully matched target bolts. However good and accurate the crossbow and however skilfully it is shot, high scores can never be attained if the bolts do not fly alike because they have not been carefully matched. Each bolt in the same set must therefore be of exactly the same length and the same weight; a heavy bolt will drop low of the group. Every feather of the fletching must be of exactly the same shape and size; large feathers will slow a bolt down. The feathers must all be glued on at the same angle; the greater the angle from straight down the shaft, the slower the bolt will fly.

Although crossbow bolts are fairly short, 12 to 14in (30 to 35cm), the point of balance can make a difference in flight. At the longer distance a bolt that is heavier in the head than the others will drop appreciably lower. The making of a high-grade set of target bolts is thus a very skilled craft.

To select the tightest grouping bolts from a set of eight, twelve or sixteen that are sold as matching, mark each bolt with a number (for example 1 to 12) and then establish an aim that will put all the bolts on a target at say 60yd (55m). Having established the aim do not adjust it but shoot the whole set of matched bolts (on a calm day) six times over, very carefully. On a separate small target face mark by number the spot where each bolt hit. If you do this carefully you will be able to mark the average 'area' of hits by each numbered bolt, disregarding, of course, the one or two bad shots with each particular bolt. With these average areas of hitting marked the six closest grouping bolts can be picked out; these will not necessarily be those grouping closest to the centre of the target, but those making the closest group with each other. If required the sights can then be adjusted to bring that group into the middle.

Plastic fletchings are of course more consistent in thickness and straighter than natural turkey feathers, but they are apt to be knocked off in shooting and this is disconcerting in a competition. Often it forces the competitor to carry a fletching jig with which to replace them.

The fletching on a bolt must be no higher than the depth of the groove; if it is the bolt will not lie properly in the groove.

Although in some cases this means that the feathers must be cut rather low, this does not matter because the shortness of the crossbow bolts and the speed at which they travel means that they need only a small fletching to keep them straight and steady in flight. For most modern crossbows the bolts must have fletching at least ¾in (2cm) from the back end of the bolt, or else the feathers may foul the catch cover.

The diameter of the bolts is another important factor. On no account must the bolt be allowed to slip forward along the groove except when the string is driving it. It must therefore be large enough in diameter to be tight under the spring until the string contacts it to drive it forward. If it were to slip forward from under the spring the string could jump over the top of the bolt instead of shooting it forward. The reason for this is that in many crossbows at full draw, the ends of the prod are above the top level of the groove in the stock so that the string begins its travel high. A similar result can occur if the back of the bolt is dome-shaped: instead of driving the bolt forward the string can slip over the top, allowing it to drop to the ground a little way off.

In a properly constructed crossbow the string should meet the back of the bolt either dead centre or slightly above centre. If the groove is so narrow and the bolt so large that the string meets it much below centre, the force of the released string can make the front of the bolt rise out of the groove and fly high, in some cases hitting the front sight. That is why some old crossbows used bolts with a short pin at the back which fitted into a ring on the string.

The Chinese used unfletched bolts in their light repeating crossbows. These had the heads and front end appreciably heavier than the back; if this were not so they would have begun to turn round in the air after travelling a short distance.

Some of the clubs practising traditional crossbow shooting on the Continent of Europe use only very strong weapons and bolts made entirely of iron or steel. Most of these bolts have no

Fig 1   Crossbowman cocking his crossbow with a metal stirrup

fletching but they do have a series of grooves at the back which lessens the weight at that end and causes them to fly straight. The front end is shaped into a screw thread. Usually one particular bolt is used in a given crossbow and is shot into a wooden target at close range, often entering the same hole. The thread on the front end of the bolts enables them to be screwed out of the target with a spanner (see page 76).

METHODS OF COCKING THE CROSSBOW

Unlike the power of a gun or rifle, which comes from an explosive charge, the power of a crossbow to project the missile comes originally from the archer's own muscles. Energy must be expended and transferred by one means or another to draw back the bowstring and cock it behind the catch.

In the days when the bows (or prods) were made of self-wood staves such as yew, ash or lancewood and were therefore comparatively weak, the drawing and cocking was usually done by

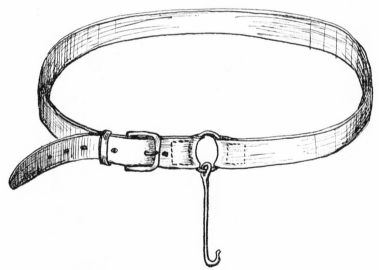

Fig 2   Belt with hook for cocking the string

26

placing both feet near the centre of the prod and pulling up against them until the string was cocked. A refinement was to fix a metal stirrup on the front of the stock so that a foot could be placed in it and the cocking made easier (see Fig 1). For heavier bows the stirrup was made big enough to take both feet. This is where the terms 'one-foot bow' or 'two-foot bow' originated. A variation of this method involved a strong hook on the belt round the waist (see Fig 2). The string was placed in the hook,

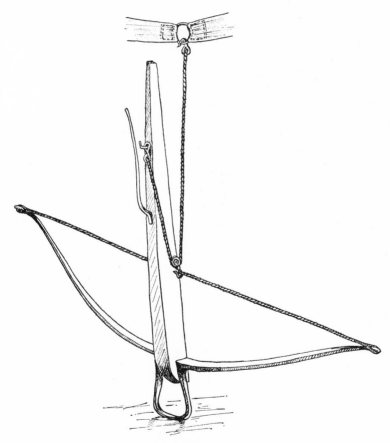

Fig 3   Crossbow with cord and pulley for cocking the string

while the foot was placed in the stirrup and pressed firmly down until the string was behind the catch. Alternatively, with the cord and pulley system, the string was attached to the hook on the pulley and drawn behind the catch as the crossbowman straightened his back (see Fig 3). Rumour has it that many a crossbowman was 'caught with his pants down' in battle owing to a faulty belt!

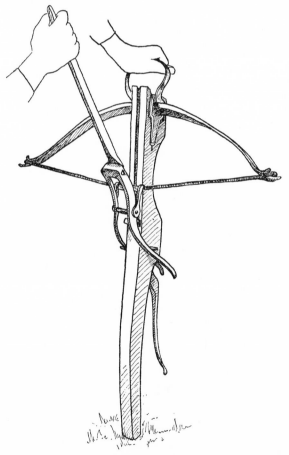

Fig 4   Crossbow with a 'goat's-foot lever' for cocking the string

28

When the stronger composite and steel prods came into use it was found essential to evolve some method of helping the archer to draw his string mechanically. The simplest aid was known as the 'goat's-foot lever' (see Fig 4). The lower part of the device engaged with pins protruding on either side of the stock; on the forward part hooks caught the string, and as the lever was drawn up and back the string dropped over the catch. In later models, and especially the stone and bullet bows of the eighteenth and

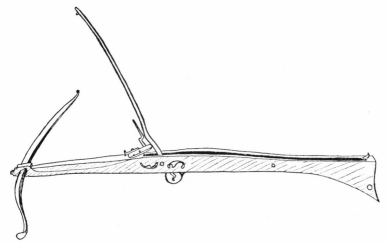

Fig 5   English bullet bow (nineteenth century) with an inbuilt cocking lever

nineteenth centuries (see page 90), this mechanism was built into the crossbow stock itself but the principle was still the same (see Fig 5 and page 36).

A more cumbersome method of cocking heavy crossbows involved a rack and cranquin. The rack hooked on to the string and had teeth that were engaged by a small gear wheel turned by a handle. As the gear was hooked on to the two pins on either side of the stock the string was drawn back and cocked (see page 53). The cranquin and rack were then removed before shooting. It seems likely that the word 'crank' comes from the same source.

Another method for drawing and cocking very heavy crossbows entailed a device called a windlass. This also had a crank handle, plus ropes and pulleys. As it was by no means easy to carry about it was no doubt used in siege situations rather than in battle and for hunting (see Fig 6 and page 53).

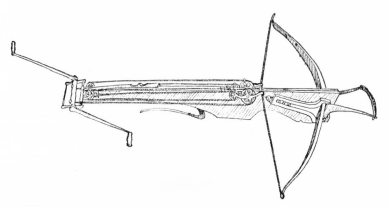

Fig 6   Crossbow with windlass attached prior to drawing the string

CROSSBOW CATCHES AND TRIGGERS

It is important for a crossbow string to be released sharply and cleanly in order to reach its maximum speed at once. If anything other than the bolt were dragged with it or even if one were to rub too hard on any part of the stock this would slow the string down. Any part of the catch mechanism that the string is designed to move when it is released should therefore be as light in weight as possible so that no energy is wasted in moving heavy catch and trigger parts.

One of the earliest catches we know was used in the very ingenious but simple Chinese repeating crossbow (see Fig 7). The ten or so unfletched bolts were carried one above the other in a magazine that was moved backwards and forwards by a

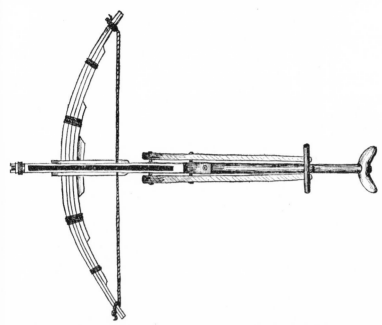

Fig 7   The Chinese repeating crossbow with bamboo prod

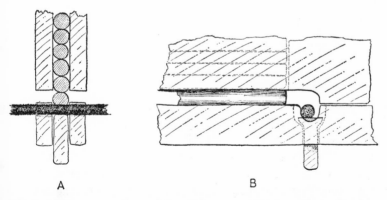

A   B

Fig 8   Two cross-sections of the Chinese repeating crossbow showing:
(A) the bolts in the magazine (seen from behind); and (B) the trigger release which pushes the string against the bolt in the groove (seen from the
side)

lever. Below the pile of bolts the magazine had a narrow channel in which the string travelled. As the lever brought the magazine forward the string was cocked by dropping into a groove at the back end of this channel, just below the rear of the next bolt to be shot. Thus when the lever pulled the magazine back again it also drew the string with it until the bow was fully drawn. At this point a piece of rod in a hole immediately beneath the string registered with the string in the groove. As the lever was brought down the piece of rod went through the hole, pushed the string out of the groove and released it behind the bolt (see Fig 8). By this method the bolts could be shot one after the other as fast as the lever could be worked back and forth. But because the bolts were not fletched they were suitable only for short-range shooting. In any case, accurate aiming was not possible because of the movement of the lever at the moment of releasing (see Fig 9).

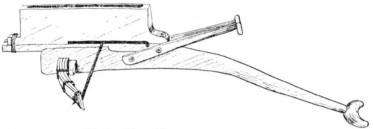

Fig 9   The Chinese repeating crossbow

For many hundreds of years and in many countries cross-bows were fitted with what is called the 'nut-and-trigger' method of release. This consisted of a thick circular disc, called the nut, which had a groove to take the string on the upper perimeter and a wedge shape cut out of the lower perimeter to take the front end of the long trigger. Usually the nut was very carefully fitted with its centre a little below the top level of the stock. No centre pin was fitted but the nut had to move freely in its hole with the assistance of some kind of grease or fat. In later examples

32

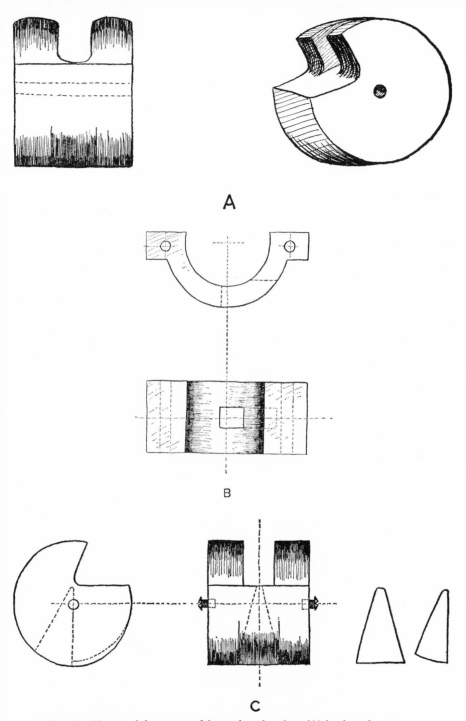

Fig 10 The revolving nut and its socket showing: (A) back and perspective views of the nut; (B) side and surface views of the socket; and (C) the 'horn nut' of the medieval crossbow and its steel wedge

a small lever stood out at the side of the stock and was used to set the nut in the right position for cocking the string. The long trigger ran almost parallel with the stock and just below it, being pressed up against a spring to release the nut (see Figs 10A, B and C).

Those who shot with this type of nut and trigger found that it had disadvantages. Being horizontal the long trigger is awkward to control with the first finger, as is usual with the modern rifle. It was therefore found best to lay the back of the butt on one's shoulder and press up the trigger with one's thumb. But this did not produce a steady aim because the upward pressure of the thumb tended to bring the bow off aim. It is, however, clear that this was the method normally used, since on many medieval crossbow stocks two grooves are cut immediately above the end of the trigger to take the first and second fingers while the thumb was on the trigger underneath.

To overcome the disadvantage of pressing upwards a subsequent improvement made it possible to release the nut by gently pulling a lever backward. The former trigger was shortened and enclosed in the stock itself. A spring-activated lever was mounted below the main trigger and caught by a small vertical trigger. A slight pull back on this second trigger released the lever, which in turn pushed up the main trigger and released the nut and string. All this rather complicated action was enclosed within the stock, except of course for the small second trigger and the lower end of the lever for recocking.

The Belgians in the nineteenth century used a slightly modified version of this action. Instead of the revolving nut catching the string from below a claw was fitted that came down over the string from above. One advantage here was that as the string was pulled back it cocked itself automatically. A two-trigger action working against springs, similar to the action described above, kept the string in position. When the small trigger was pulled back or squeezed the claw was lifted and the string released. This method of pulling the trigger 'back' instead of 'up'

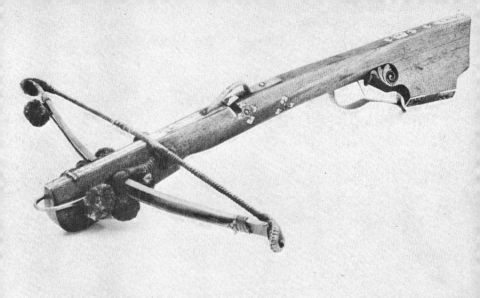

Page 35 (*above*) German sporting crossbow with a safety cord on the prod in case of breakage; (*below*) Flemish mid-seventeenth-century crossbow with steel prod (the nut is inserted back to front by mistake)

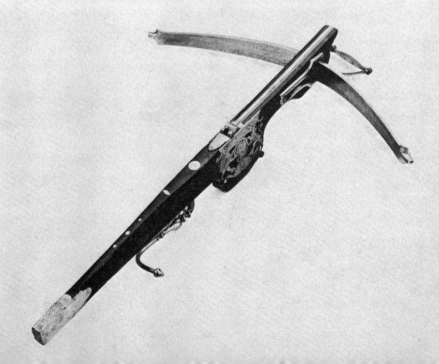

Page 36 (*above*) Belgian nineteenth-century crossbow with claw latch and side pins for 'goat's-foot lever'; (*below*) East European sporting crossbow with an inbuilt cocking lever and steel prod (eighteenth century)

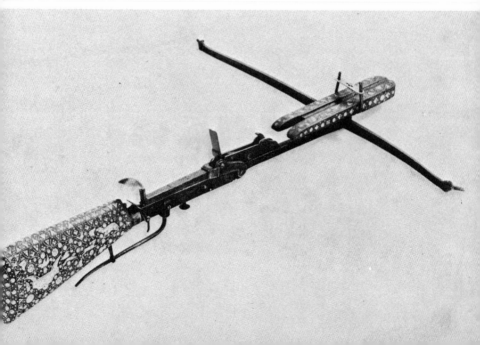

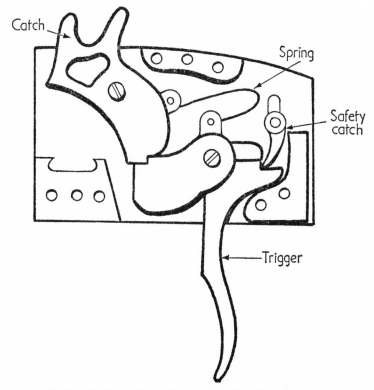

Fig 11   (A) Crossbow trigger and latch with safety catch

eventually resulted in the butt being altered so that it could be held against one's shoulder and lower down instead of resting on top of one's shoulder.

Most modern crossbows have simpler catches and triggers but they are still based on the principle of the old nut and trigger, though of course with the trigger curving down vertically (see Fig 11A). Both catch and trigger are held on steel pins and the surfaces in contact are case hardened and polished to give smooth movement in spite of the heavy pressure borne by the catch. When the bowstring is pulled back along the stock it pushes back point A, brings point B up into position and cocks

37

the string by allowing point C on the trigger to engage the catch by the action of the spring D. By a steady pull on the trigger it comes to the point where it trips the catch and releases the string (see Fig 12).

As long as the contacting surfaces of the trigger and catch are hard metal and polished for smooth movement the remaining portions of these parts can be light alloy or even hardwood. If they are all steel the movement of the catch can be speeded up

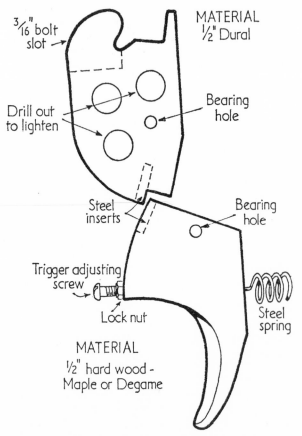

Fig 11   (B) Trigger and catch as used on US crossbows

by drilling a few large holes away from the working surfaces in order to lighten the part and speed up the movement.

Some catches hold the string on two points so that the bolt is in contact with the string before it is released. Others hold the string on one point only. As the catch revolves the string is fed on to the back of the bolt and gives it a tremendous 'prod'.

CHAPTER 2

Shooting Technique

Shooting a modern crossbow is in many ways similar to shooting a rifle, but there are differences.

For instance, there is virtually no recoil with a crossbow so that provided you hold it steadily while you release it there is no need to hold the butt hard into your shoulder. As with rifle shooting there is of course an advantage in shooting kneeling or prone so that your left elbow can be supported on your knee or on the ground. I personally prefer the kneeling position, especially for tranquillising animals, because it is usually possible to remain kneeling to recock the weapon whereas to shoot prone wastes time and effort.

Once you have zeroed the sights (ie adjusted the sights by trial and error for the expected distance to be shot) and selected the appropriate type of bolts or darts the next step is to cock the string and take up the position for shooting (standing, kneeling or prone). It is not until then that you should place the bolt in the breech. If a safety catch is fitted this must be turned to the 'shoot' position. If you are using open sights, say for target shooting, you must bring up the blade of the front sight level with and midway between the shoulders of the rear sight. Now bring this 'picture' level with the bottom of the bull's-eye on the target.

Up to this point normal breathing is sufficient but you should now take a fairly deep breath, half exhale it and hold until the shot has been completed. This lessens body movement during the shot.

Because the full pull of the string is held by the catch in a crossbow, the trigger is usually much harder to pull than a rifle trigger, which has only the pin to control. It is therefore essential to train yourself to hold the aim right on the bull while you pull the trigger very steadily back until it releases the string. The surfaces of the catch and trigger should be highly polished and greased but will still need some effort to pull the trigger. This means that you may be tempted to pull the trigger with a jerk directly the aim is on the mark, instead of steadily squeezing the trigger while you hold the aim on the centre. You are thus less likely to jerk the bow off aim.

When you can neither kneel nor lie prone, but must stand erect to shoot, as in competitive target shooting, it is a help to rest your left elbow just above your hip-joint and close into your body with the stock held just in front of the trigger guard. Your feet should be well apart to give a steady stance. Even then real steadiness of aim on the target can be developed only by continual practice and concentration. You must practise the habit of holding on aim right through the act of squeezing the trigger so that you are still on aim, without relaxing at all, when the bolt hits the target. The idea is to achieve a sort of mental 'follow through'.

If, in target practice, the whole group of hits is positioned in the same direction off the centre, the trouble is likely to be either a strong wind or incorrect zeroing of the sights. If on the other hand the hits are spread on both sides of the target, you are more likely to be troubled by unsteadiness in squeezing the trigger.

If you are using a strong prod the centre of the string is unlikely to be pulled out of line with the centre of the channel (or 'barrel') on the stock, for it will centre itself as soon as it is placed on the catch. But if the string is pulled slightly sideways in hand-cocking a weak prod, it may remain out of true and when released may shoot the bolt slightly to one side. Care should therefore be taken to pull the string straight back when hand-cocking. A centre mark on the string may help you to get it always in line with the channel. In addition it is best to place three fingers of each hand on the string with each first finger just touching the side of the stock so that you give an even pull straight back to the catch.

If a stirrup is not fitted to the crossbow and you find it uncomfortable to pull back with the butt in your stomach you can generally drill a $\frac{5}{16}$in (8mm) hole through the front of the stock so that a loop of strong cord can be fixed through it. It must be long enough to go under the instep and allow the prod to be cocked by pulling upwards against the loop.

No crossbow should ever be loosed without a bolt in the groove. The recoil of the limbs is so fast that without the damping down effect of a bolt the sudden stop creates such a shock that irreparable damage can be done to the prod. This may not show in a break at once but it may well lead to one later.

CLOUT SHOOTING

As crossbows have a good long cast and can be accurately aimed clout shooting is an appropriate type of shooting for which to use them. The term 'clout shooting' comes from the name given by the English longbowmen to their method of practising for warfare. It was essential for them to know exactly how much their bow had to be elevated to reach a given distance, because in battle the Captain of the Archers would give a distance according to the number of paces needed in his judgement to reach the enemy. For instance, he might shout 'Eight score!' 160yd (146m) and then 'Loose!' Thus all the arrows would reach the enemy at once. In practice, for instance on the village green, archers would throw down a white cloth (a clout), step say, 160 paces from it, turn round and try to hit it. The modern equivalent is a small target marked on the ground, in the centre of which is a small white-covered straw boss propped up to make it visible.

The official distance for clout shooting in both England and North America is 180yd (165m) for men and 140yd (128m) for women. The target is 24ft (7·31m) across and is made up of a central white boss that is 2ft 6in (76·2cm) in diameter and is propped up at 45° from the ground in the centre of a 3ft (91·5cm) ring. Outside this marked on the ground are rings at 6ft (1·88m), 12ft (3·66m), 18ft (5·5m) and 24ft (7·31m). The clout (or boss) itself counts 6 points; the 3ft ring (on the ground) counts 5 points, the 6ft ring 4 points, the 12ft ring 3 points, the 18ft ring 2 points and the 24ft ring 1 point.

If it is impractical to mark out the actual ground a rope can be used as a substitute though this is not quite so satisfying to shoot at. The rope must have a ring or loop at one end and bindings or knots at 1ft 6in (45·72cm), 3ft, 6ft, 9ft (2·8m) and 12ft. To check the score, the loop is placed on a centre peg in the ground and the rope is stretched and taken round in a circle rather like a compass. The bolts that fall within a given ring are placed together at that distance from the centre so that they can be claimed by those who shot them when the scores are recorded.

One problem in clout shooting with crossbows is the difficulty that may arise in spotting where the bolt has fallen in order to correct the sight. Two aids in this connection are strong field glasses and a volunteer standing level with the target, but at a safe distance, who can indicate to the archer the spot where his bolts hit. Bright crestings on the bolts are a help too.

The shooting is often done in two directions to save time. And a round consists of thirty-six bolts.

FIELD SHOOTING

The American longbowmen who enjoyed the opportunity of hunting big game in the winter season devised a special form of shooting for practice during the rest of the year. Known as field shooting, it consists of placing targets of various sizes at varying distances from 10yd (9·14m) to 80yd (73·14m), and in terrain as much like hunting country as possible (see page 54). This official field course, as it is called, has been adopted by the governing body of international archery, the FITA, and by that of English archery, the GNAS (Grand National Archery Society). In England more and more crossbowmen are finding it possible to shoot round these field courses with longbowmen (see Appendix 2 for rules).

FLIGHT SHOOTING

Shooting purely to attain distance rather than at a target represents a fascinating hobby for some crossbowmen. It involves not only finding the best possible equipment for the purpose but also practising the right technique under the most suitable conditions.

Let's look first at the question of equipment. Unless you are in close touch with a professional bowyer who is prepared to experiment and has the time to do so, you will do better to learn how to make your own composite prods. After initial practice on a straight prod (see page 58) you would be able to construct a stronger recurved prod especially for flight shooting. In the course of experiments to achieve the best results you may well go too near the safety margin and have a breakage, but it is easy and cheap enough to repair the damage or construct a new prod on safer lines.

The first objective is to construct a prod with the fastest moving limbs that can be held satisfactorily in the stock. Other factors being equal, the lighter the limb the faster it will move. If you weigh sheet fibreglass laminate against the same volume of seasoned maple wood you will find that the fibreglass is heavier. The proportion of fibreglass to wood must therefore be kept as low as possible. A very thin core and a lot of thick fibreglass must be avoided, as this is where a lot of bowyers make their mistake. On the other hand the fibreglass on the belly and the back must be strong enough to control the wood core and act as a 'stress skin'. This is where experimentation comes in.

Another point concerning the prod must be borne in mind: the shorter the limb the faster it will move; but if it is too short it will not take the required bend without breaking.

It is therefore best to start long, say 3ft (91·5cm) for a 14in (35cm) draw, and work down an inch off each limb each time until you reach the limit—or pass it! The amount of recurve is another matter that will affect speed. For flight prods a little more recurve than the target prods carry is an advantage. You must of course regulate this during construction by putting a greater curve on the ends of the former, over which the prod is glued.

The next point to consider is how to fix the prod in the stock to avoid the friction of the string and the bolt on the groove. Some flight shooters anchor the centre of the prod above the groove of the stock, so that the string does not press down on the top of the groove at any point. This involves special plates screwed on to the sides of the stock, so that the bolt can pass underneath the prod. The centre of the prod must be strong enough to allow for a section to be cut out so as to enable the bolt to pass cleanly. Another method entails setting the prod partly below the groove at a slight angle, again with a section cut out to avoid weakening the front of the stock. Here the prod is almost a 'centre shot' and the rubbing of the string on the groove is reduced to a minimum. To make things easier the top of the groove can be lightly oiled, although it will of course already be highly polished.

For flight shooting the string must be as light as possible commensurate with safety. Unfortunately the strongest thread (Dacron), is slightly elastic; to get the most power out of a bow you need a string with no stretch at all, such as linen. For strength per weight, however, Terylene or Dacron offer the best solution.

We now come to the bolt. Here a good deal of experimenting needs to be done to discover the best shape and weight. Aerodynamics must definitely be brought in here. Fletchings are certainly needed but they must be thin yet stiff and as small as possible. Cut-down plastic fletchings are best for flight bolts. In addition the shaft of the bolt should be polished to minimise friction in flight, and painted some very bright colour, such as Dayglo; if this is not done it will be very difficult to find, even in short-cut grass or on a smooth sandy beach.

Mathematicians have worked out that 43° above horizontal is the angle that will give the longest shot, other factors being equal. Yet a head wind or a following wind must inevitably affect the best angle under those circumstances. Getting the angle of the shot right is so important that it is worth while rigging up a marker of some sort under the stock giving an angle of 43° from the level of the bolt groove. A plumbline hanging down loose will indicate when the correct angle is reached. As you are not likely to be able to see this indicator while you are shooting ask someone else to tell you when the angle is right. (In any case a patient assistant is very useful in flight shooting as he or she can act as a witness to check the distances. Furthermore, when you are looking for bolts four eyes are always better than two.)

A stock made for flight shooting should be heavy and the butt should be held rigidly into your shoulder at the moment of loosing so that there is no backward 'give' to reduce the forward thrust of the prod.

Having found a suitable place and decided on the best direction to shoot, mark out the ground with a peg at every 100yd or 100m interval and then shoot along the line of pegs, taking any likely wind drift into consideration. The best conditions for long shots are dry clear air, a following wind and a time of day when no people are about. (See page 126 for American Flight Rules.)

BOLT VELOCITY

An American crossbowman, Weytus Dewey of Los Angeles,

46

wrote to the editor of *Chit Chat*, the magazine of the crossbow-men of America, saying: 'I've figured out an easy way to determine bolt velocity and want to pass it along.'

His method was to mark a horizontal line near the top of the target and as nearly as possible on the same level as the barrel when shooting. Then with the front and rear sights set at the same height from the stock he started shooting close to the target, and moved back until the shafts were hitting exactly 1ft (30·48cm) below the point aimed at. Remember that, neglecting air resistance, the arrow during flight obeys the laws of falling bodies; it will therefore drop a distance *s* equal to the product of one-half *g*, the acceleration of gravity, times the square of the time of flight *t*. Expressed mathematically the formula runs:

$$s = \frac{g}{2} \times t^2$$

Since we know that *s*, the distance fallen through by the arrow, is 1ft and that *g* is close to 32ft (9·75m) per second per second, the value of *t* is readily found, thus:

$$1 = \frac{32}{2} \times t^2$$

Whence $t^2 = \frac{1}{16}$ and $t = \frac{1}{4}$ second

Let us suppose that our distance from the target when the arrows were hitting exactly 1ft below the mark was *d*ft (*d*cm). Then, since the arrow travelled *d*ft, horizontally, in $\frac{1}{4}$ second (neglecting additional air resistance over the increased distance) it would have travelled $4 \times d$ in one full second. Hence, the 'average velocity' of the arrow while travelling the distance *d* was $4 \times d$ft per second.

Greater accuracy would be achieved if you were to move back until the shafts were hitting 4ft (1·22m) below the point of aim, instead of only 1ft. In this case, again using the formula, the time of flight *t* will be close on $\frac{1}{2}$ second, and the average velocity will be twice the new distance from the target.

Comment from Mr F. Isles:

The beauty of Weytus's Method, aside from its great simplicity is that it yields true 'average velocities' for the distance shot, and not simply 'muzzle velocities' as usually determined by chronograph or ballistic pendulum.

The Dewey Method takes air resistance throughout the trajectory fully into account. Thus the velocities so determined, while decreasing, due to air resistance, as increasingly longer distances are shot, are the true average velocities with a margin of error of about 1 per cent. This slight error arises from the assumption that g, the acceleration of gravity, is a round 32ft (9·75m), rather than the actual 32·2ft (9·81m) per second per second and from the fact that no allowance has been made for the arrow falling vertically through the distance between the mark and the point of impact a trifle more slowly than it would in a perfect vacuum. We have also neglected to allow for the slight distance between the line-of-sight through the crossbow sights and the axis of the arrow shaft when it rests in the barrel-groove; for total accuracy this should be deducted, in all cases, from the distance of fall s.

Here are two simple examples of how this method of calculation can be put to use:

1 With a weak prod at 20yd (18·28m). This would give the 'average velocity' as $4 \times 60\text{ft} = 240\text{ft}$ (73·14m) per second, or about 165mph (264km/h).

2 With a much stronger prod to give a 1ft drop at 30yd (27·42m). This would give the 'average velocity' as $4 \times 90\text{ft} = 360\text{ft}$ (111·18m) per second, or about 245mph (392km/h).

CROSSBOW DARTS

As in archery club shooting it is sometimes a welcome relaxation for crossbowmen to participate in a shooting game. Crossbow darts, for instance, can give rise to keen competition between well-matched teams. Paper faces drawn on the same pattern as a standard darts board but slightly larger can be obtained (see Useful Addresses, page 136).

A distance for shooting appropriate to the prowess of the

teams can be agreed upon and the competition can be conducted according to the usual scoring method and rules of the game. Three bolts are used instead of three darts.

I should like to offer one word of advice from my experience in this game, as to how to make the target face last longer. Before pinning the face to the straw boss, cut the ring of numbers away from the scoring segments and fix the two parts on the boss independently. This means that when the 'treble-top' has been shot to pieces the scoring segments can be turned round to a fresh position without any need to shift the numbers.

CHAPTER 3

Make Your Own Crossbow

THE STOCK

It has been mentioned in a previous chapter that the essential factor for accuracy in a crossbow is that the stock, especially the bolt groove, should be straight. This is very difficult to ensure if you use a solid board of say, 1$\frac{3}{16}$in (3cm) thickness, because of the possibility of warping. I therefore suggest that three $\frac{3}{8}$in (1cm) boards should be used and glued together so that the centre board has the grain running vertically and the two outer boards have the grain running horizontally. There are two other advantages in using this method to form the stock. If a small bandsaw is not available the $\frac{3}{8}$in boards can easily be shaped with a coping saw before being glued together. The mortice for the trigger mechanism and the bolt groove can be formed by leaving the centre board blank where required.

As to the best woods to use for the stock, for appearance a good choice would be walnut or mahogany (known as sapele), both of which are easy to work and take a good polish. Well-seasoned beech is easier to obtain and is also reliable, but it looks better if it is stained before polishing.

Three boards 3ft × 8in × $\frac{3}{8}$in (91·5cm × 20cm × 1cm) are required. If you are handy with a plane, however, the lower 2in (5cm) of the butt can be cut from spare wood, which will make it possible to use boards 6in (15cm) wide instead of 8in.

The shape of the stock should first be marked out on 1in

50

squared paper (see the heavy line on Fig 12), the pattern is then transferred to the two outer boards by means of carbon paper and cut out with a small bandsaw or coping saw. The centre board, which will have the grain placed vertically, should then be cut into the required lengths so as to avoid the spaces taken by the trigger mortice and the upper groove.

The surfaces to be glued should be coarse sanded and brushed thoroughly to remove any dust, then coated with a fairly strong glue, such as Laytex wood-working adhesive. Before the glue gets too tacky the various pieces of the centre board must be placed together correctly and the two outer boards carefully registered. Placing the stock on paper on the floor or a flat table top and evenly distributing plenty of heavy weights over it may give sufficient pressure for a satisfactory glue joint, but four or six G-cramps with straight battens would make a better job. Take care not to screw the cramps on to the stock surface without protection.

If the centre boards have not been completely shaped before gluing they must be cut level with the outer boards when the glue is well set. Then all edges except the bolt groove must be rounded with a rasp or coarse file. The top of this bolt groove must be perfectly flat and smooth, so any unevenness should be carefully planed and strips of Formica glued on to give a long straight gap of $\frac{3}{16}$in (0·5cm) width down the dead centre. The smoothness of Formica makes a good surface on which the bolt and string can ride. Sharp edges should be rounded. The entire surface of the stock should now be fine sanded and painted all over with a clear wood filler. When the filler is hard another thorough sanding should be given and two or three coats of clear varnish or polyurethane applied.

The middle of the stock must be kept deep to protect the fingers and thumb of the left hand from being caught by the string. To improve the grip as well as the appearance a $\frac{9}{16}$in (1·5cm) wide groove should be cut parallel with the bottom edge, its centre about 1$\frac{1}{4}$in from the bottom. This groove can start on both sides about 2in from the trigger guard and run forward for about 5 to 6in (12 to 15cm). A sharp gouge is of course the best tool for this job.

The trigger and catch should be made of $\frac{5}{16}$in or $\frac{3}{8}$in (8 or 9mm) tool steel and case hardened, at least on the parts that have mutual contact. If the shape of the trigger and catch as shown in Fig 12 is used, care must be taken to round the upper left-hand surface of the trigger slightly to a radius of 1in. This surface must be polished before it is case hardened so that no roughness is felt when the trigger is pulled under pressure. The pins holding the trigger and catch should be made of $\frac{1}{4}$in (6mm) bright steel and must be carefully positioned, otherwise the mechanism will not function properly and may become dangerous.

The trigger cover must also be carefully made to exact dimensions in order to prevent the string from jumping over the catch before it has been properly loosed. The dotted line in Fig 12 indicates the depth of the groove underneath the cover which takes the bolt-holding spring. Two diamond-shaped plates of Formica can be fixed to the sides of the stock with a single screw each, in such a position that they cover the two pins and keep them in place.

The bolt-holding spring can be made from half a normal mortice-lock spring, which is usually shaped like a wide open V. If the two limbs are separated by cutting through the centre circle leaving a half circle on each limb, the larger limb can be drilled and fixed in the catch cover groove so that a complete semicircle is forward of the cover and will hold the bolt down in the breech.

The prod cover can be made of the same $\frac{3}{8}$in thick wood as the stock. It is best to fix this with two wing nuts and bolts to the stock so that the prod can be easily dismantled when required. Otherwise it will have to be screwed on.

The front sight can be a blade made of a small bolt protruding from an inverted U shape made of mild steel strip, drilled and screwed to the side of the stock an inch or two from the forward

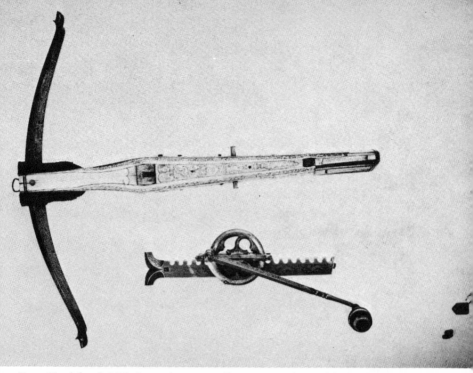

Page 53 (*above*) Mid-sixteenth century German crossbow with a gold damascened steel prod and rack and cranquin cocking device; (*below*) European crossbow with a windlass cocking device

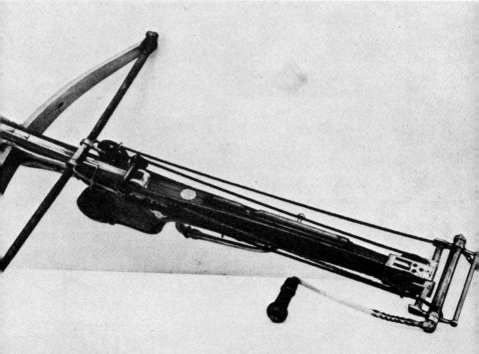

Page 54   Field shooting with coloured animal targets

end, and of course high enough to give plenty of room for the bolt and its feathers to pass underneath.

The rear sight must have some means of considerable adjustment vertically and also a slight adjustment laterally, for windage and so on. A simple way of doing this is to provide a metal tube about 4in (10cm) long and $\frac{5}{16}$in in diameter. If one end is plugged with wood a small hole can be drilled in it to take a screw to fix the V sight. This can be made of $\frac{5}{8}$in (1·5cm) mild steel strip about $\frac{5}{16}$in wide. By bending this strip in half at right angles, you can drill and counter-sink one part to take the fixing screw, while a $\frac{1}{16}$in (2mm) deep hacksaw-cut in the dead centre of the other part will make a good rear sight similar to the modern target pistol aperture. If a V is preferred this can be cut with a small triangular file. A hole just wide enough to take the rear sight tube must be drilled in front of the rear screw of the catch cover. This hole should go vertically down through the catch cover and the stock for about $3\frac{1}{2}$in (9cm). To secure this rear sight tube at the required height a fixing bolt with a knurled head should be screwed through a hole in the side of the stock. A square or hexagonal head will work of course, but the thread should be fine to make a good locking bolt.

Flat black paint is best for front and back sights to avoid highlights when aiming. The shoulders of the back sight can now be locked with the screw at about $2\frac{1}{2}$in (6cm) from the level of the catch cover, which should be sufficient for a fair distance. Should there be a certain amount of wind drift the back sight can be locked slightly to the right or left without the aperture closing completely. If you prefer a more elaborate pair of sights or a telescopic sight these can be obtained from the dealers mentioned on page 136

THE COMPOSITE PROD

As a beginning it is best to make a straight-limbed composite prod. This, as mentioned in a previous chapter, is constructed of a wooden core with strips of special sheet fibreglass laminate glued to both sides. The gluing process requires considerable pressure and a temperature of at least 100° F (38° C) for about five hours. If therefore at least four strong G-cramps and an airing cupboard or some other place capable of being raised to 100° F are not available it will be necessary to buy a suitable composite prod from a dealer (see page 136). Alloy or steel prods can be purchased but I do not advise their use because metal fatigue can cause them to shatter, with pieces of metal flying about at high speed. Trial prods can be made of seasoned ash or hickory but these can only be very weak or they will snap.

To construct a straight-limbed composite prod suitable for the stock already described the following materials will be needed:

1 Two laminations of well-seasoned straight-grained wood, 16⅛in (41cm) long by 1⅜in (4cm) wide and tapered from ⅛in to 1/16in (3mm to 2mm) thick. Rock (or Canadian) maple is best, but no doubt ash or hickory would also do for the core.

2 Two strips of 'Bo-tuf' fibreglass laminate. These should be at least 32in (81·5cm) long, at least 1⅜in (4cm) wide and can be either 40thou or 50thou thick. This material is made only in North America but it can also be bought in Britain (see page 136).

3 At least ¼lb (100gm) of 'Urac 185' glue plus separate hardener powder. This is a CIBA product and can be bought in small quantities (see page 136). Unfortunately no other glue will adequately stick fibreglass for the purpose.

If a small planing machine is not available to taper the wood laminations this can be done on a belt or drum sander with care and constant measuring. On the thick end of both laminations a ⅜in chamfer must be sanded so that these two ends overlap flush for the complete ⅜in. Both sides of these wood laminations must now be scratched to give a good 'key'. This is best done with a hacksaw blade held in two hands. A stiff brush should be used to clear the dust.

About ⅛lb (55gm) of glue should be sufficient for our purpose. This should be mixed in a glass jar with the correct proportion of the hardener according to directions. A wooden rod or spatula is best for this job. Next lift a corner of the protective strip from the fibreglass sheets and pull it off to reveal the rough gluing surface. Take care not to finger that surface of the fibreglass after the strip is pulled off.

Now you are ready to start gluing. Have ready a 3ft (91·5cm) long piece of straight batten, say 3⅛in × 4in (8cm × 10cm) on which you have placed a strip of polythene sheet wide enough to cover the surface. Cover the rough side of one piece of fibreglass with glue and place it, glue up, on the batten; cover both sides of each wood lamination with glue and place them on the fibreglass with the chamfered ends overlapping in the middle. Likewise coat the rough side of the remaining fibreglass sheet and register this with the other fibreglass and wood laminations. Another piece of polythene should be placed on the fibreglass before another batten (which can be thinner) is placed on top.

To aid the cramping, the lower batten can be rested on two pieces of thick wood or the open end of a box. When tightening the cramps (4, 6 or 8) make sure that the laminations do not slide out of register. If the cramps are large enough additional wood to spread the pressure evenly is a help.

As glue will be pressed out the laminations should lie flat while they are in the improvised oven. The temperature should be kept at over 100° F for five hours. When cured, the glue should be allowed to cool slowly and then the laminations uncramped. The edges of the glue will be sharp so must be handled carefully.

As with the shape of the stock, mark out the shape of the prod on 1in squared paper from the pattern on page 58, Fig 12.

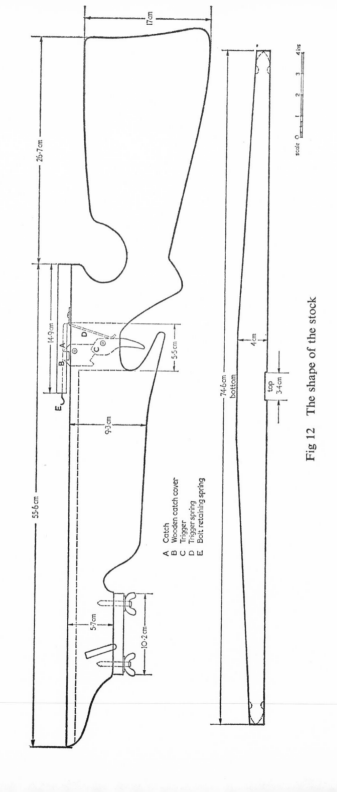

17cm

26·7cm

14·9cm

5·5cm

9·3cm

55·6cm

5·7cm

10·2cm

A Catch
B Wooden catch cover
C Trigger
D Trigger spring
E Bolt retaining spring

74·6cm
bottom

4cm

top
3·4cm

scale 0 1 2 3 4ins

Fig 12 The shape of the stock

You will notice that one edge is straight while the other edge tapers from about 3⅛in from the centre line to the two ends. The centre line should be drawn across just at the centre of the overlapping joint. Having drawn the outline full size on 1in squared paper, cut this shape out and place it on the fibreglass laminate. With a sharp pencil draw carefully round the paper and cut out the prod with a bandsaw or sharp hacksaw blade. The heavy lines show that the ends of the prod are cut square. This is so that 1½in long reinforcing pieces can be glued on to the forward side of each end before the nock is cut. Provided the surface of the fibreglass is roughened with coarse sandpaper these pieces of wood, say ⅛in thick, can be glued on with an epoxy resin adhesive and should be under pressure for about eight hours. After this the ends can be rounded and the nocks (notches) cut in the positions shown (see Fig 12). Cut the nocks and sand them in such a way that no sharp or rough edges are left to wear the string unduly.

If the wood laminations have been carefully made to the thickness and width of the tapers given above the limbs should not be out of tiller when the string is fitted, that is, one limb stiffer than the other. This would cause inaccuracy and must be corrected. To check the tiller mark a spot at about mid-limb, the same distance from the centre on both limbs. Then measure the length of a line that crosses the string at right angles and passes through this spot. If the distance from that spot to the string is shorter in one limb than the other, that limb is too stiff and must be corrected. After marking this limb take off the string and reduce the width of the limb by filing away first the edge of the fibreglass and then the wood core on the lower tapering edge. Do not touch the straight top of the limb or the surface of the glass. Reduce the width gradually for the whole length of the one limb and repeatedly test for tiller until both limbs bend equally. After that sand the edges, not the surface of the fibreglass, and coat all the wood with two coats of clear varnish.

It only remains for the prod to be fitted tightly into the slot in the stock. The recess on top of the prod goes in first, but not before a padding of leather or felt has been glued into the slot so that the prod is held tightly but does not touch bare wood anywhere.

Using 50thou fibreglass the above method should make about a 50lb (24kg) prod; if you are using 40thou fibreglass the pull should be between 30 and 40lb (13 and 18kg). Being of composite construction this will be quite speedy enough for target shooting at 60yd (55m) or for small game hunting.

THE SHOOTING STRING

The greatest strain on a bowstring comes not when the string is cocked at full draw but as the bolt leaves the prod and the two limbs snap the string taut. At that moment a 50lb (24kg) prod can put a sudden strain of 200lb (96kg) on a string. It is therefore essential to allow plenty of margin in the strength of a bowstring. Against that requirement we must remember that the heavier the string the slower the speed at which the bolt will travel and the shorter the distance attained. Careful tests have established that the speed of the bolt is reduced by the equivalent of adding one-third of the weight of the string to the weight of the bolt. So unnecessary weight of string should be avoided, especially in flight shooting.

The choice of material for the string is of course important. It must have as little stretch as possible. For this reason nylon is not suitable, while cotton does not have enough strength. Of natural fibres linen is the best. Hemp is good but not so easily obtainable. Terylene (also sold under the American name of Dacron) is the strongest but is more expensive.

You can obtain the strength of the complete string by ascertaining the breaking strain of one thread and then taking enough threads to make the required total breaking strain (the average breaking strain of thread is sometimes marked on the spool). Otherwise you can ascertain it like this: carefully suspend one thread by binding it round a rod so that there is no sharp bend in the thread and then add weights until breaking point is reached, or pull down with a spring balance until the thread breaks. You should do this three or four times to get an average weight.

The overall length of the string (ie between the far ends of the loops) should be 2 to 2½in (5 to 6cm) shorter than the distance between the nocks of the prod (assuming the normal prod to be 28 to 36in (80 to 90cm) between nocks). A piece of board about the same length as the prod will be needed and in this must be fixed two pegs 3in (7·5cm) long and about ½in (1·25cm) in diameter. On one peg loosely tie one end of the thread, then wind round from peg to peg until you have the required number of threads (half the number on each side of the pegs). Now tie the two ends together in a reef knot. You now have one continuous circle of thread running round the pegs. With a pencil make a mark on each section of the threads at B 1in from each peg (see Fig 13). Then slip the threads round until the marks come opposite each other at the centre of the board. The threads between these marks will become the loops to go over the nocks of the prod, so some whipping or serving must be put on between the two marks on each section. The string will look better if this serving is done with thin coloured string or heavy thread. Red or green look particularly well.

The served parts are then slid back to the pegs and adjusted evenly round them. Using the same string or thread as for the serving, bind the sections together for about 2in (5cm), thus forming the loops C (see Fig 14). The string can now be taken off the pegs. It should be twisted a few times before being put on the prod. As this type of string has fixed loops at both ends any adjustment must be done by twisting or untwisting. Normally an adjustment of about ½in can be effected in this way.

As there are only half the number of threads in the loops, it might seem that these would be weak spots and would lead to breaks, but experience has shown that breakages usually occur at the nocking point and not at the loops.

All that remains to complete the string is to rub it well with beeswax and then with a piece of leather doubled over to melt the beeswax into the string (see Fig 13). This is done with the prod braced.

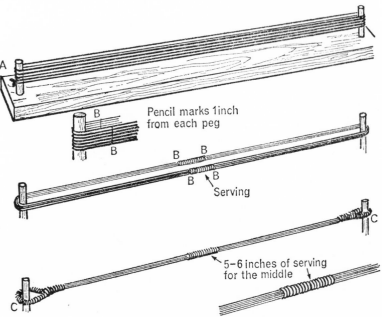

Fig 13   Making a bowstring

Before the prod is used it is wise to 'serve' or bind the centre of the string with strong thread, with the end well waxed. A different colour from the string looks well. Start the serving (as at A in Fig 14) 1in from the centre when the prod is braced and continue binding in the direction as at B for 2in. Finish by pulling the thread back through several loops as at C. This serving will protect the string from being worn by the catch.

If the prod is too strong to be bent by hand sufficiently to fit the string in the nocks, two extra nocks will have to be cut nearer the ends of the prod than the main nocks. A secondary string must then be made long enough to fit easily into these secondary nocks. After the main string has been looped over each limb of the prod, when it is fitted in the stock, the secondary string can be fitted into the outside nocks and this string pulled back and cocked. This process should bend the prod sufficiently for the main string to be fitted. After which the secondary string can be taken off and put aside.

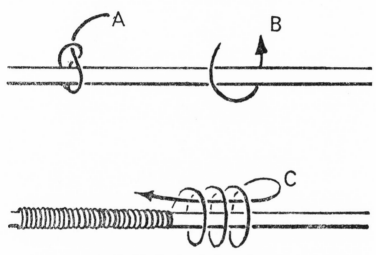

Fig 14   Serving the bowstring

THE BOLTS

A bolt must be as straight as possible. As already mentioned, a set of six or more bolts for target shooting should be as closely matched as possible in weight, spine (springiness) and balance. To obtain these requirements to perfection takes the professional fletcher all his time and skill. Nevertheless with care amateurs can produce quite satisfactory bolts.

The simplest way to make a serviceable bolt is to obtain

straight birch or ramin dowel rods $\frac{5}{16}$in (8mm) in diameter from a timber merchant. They are fairly cheap. The straightest and roundest should be chosen; if they are slightly bent they can usually be straightened by hand, although sometimes heat will be needed. After cutting the rod to the correct length, say 12 to 15in (30 to 35cm), rub it smooth with sandpaper. Rough edges should be cleaned and the end of the shaft rubbed with sandpaper.

MAKING THE PILE

A first-class brass pile (point for target shooting) can be made quite simply from $\frac{5}{16}$in outside diameter brass tubing of 26 gauge with a short length of $\frac{9}{32}$in (7mm) brass rod sweated into the front end with solder. Cut a 1in length of tubing and a $\frac{1}{2}$in (1·25cm) length of rod. After cleaning carefully with emery cloth to obtain bright metal surfaces on both metal parts, smear them with flux and heat with gas or a blowlamp; when they are sufficiently hot coat the rod with solder. Before the solder cools insert two-thirds of the rod into the tube and leave to cool.

A breast- or hand-drill held in a vice can be used to spin the pile while you are filing it to a point; a threaded rod that will screw tightly into the open end of the pile is a convenient way of holding the pile in the chuck of the drill while you are filing and finishing. Emery cloth or sandpaper will give a good finish if you use it while the pile is turning in the drill. All piles are best fitted by using resin. When the shaft has been carefully shaped to fit right down into the pile, put a few pieces of resin in the pile and hold it over the lighted gas until the resin melts, but take care not to melt the solder. Insert the shaft right home and see that it is on straight before the resin cools; clean off the surplus resin and finally polish up the pile with emery cloth.

DEAL BOLTS

The best wooden bolts are made from very well-seasoned deal boards with straight grain. These are sawn lengths $\frac{3}{8}$in (1cm) square, an inch or so longer than the required bolt. With a sharp plane each edge is taken off in turn until the shaft is very nearly round. This operation is easier if you use a board or piece of batten, say 20in (51cm) long, with a straight V groove cut along it. A small nail is driven into the groove at one end as a stop. The square shaft is placed in the groove and the planing is then quite simple. A hollow beading plane makes a rounder finish. The rounding of the shaft is completed with sandpaper.

MAKING A FOOTING

Deal and ramin shafts are liable to break if they hit a hard object. If they are to withstand hard usage it is therefore wise to splice on a 'footing' of hardwood. This is not difficult for anyone used to handling tools. The footing should be of degame or some other straight-grained hardwood; a piece 6in (15cm) long by $\frac{3}{8}$in square is best. Make a fine saw cut with the grain, exactly down the centre for 4in (10cm). Draw a pencil line exactly across the centre of the end of the deal shaft, also with the grain, then plane a 4in taper from each side to the pencil line B (Fig 15). Next bind the footing with a few turns of thread just at the end of the saw cut to prevent splitting. Glue the taper and force it into the saw cut, making the two shafts line up straight. Bind with cord until the glue is thoroughly dry. After this plane off the protruding ears until the footing is the same diameter ($\frac{5}{16}$in) as the deal shaft, and finish with sandpaper.

FLETCHING

The bolts will now require three feathers glued on for steering purposes. This is rather a difficult job to do properly, for naturally if the vanes are not put on straight the bolt will not fly true but will wobble or 'flirt'. It is wise to mark out the shaft in pencil first, as at E (Fig 15). D is a line round the shaft about 1in (2·5cm) from the end, and C a line 1$\frac{9}{16}$in (4cm) from D, allowing for feathers 1$\frac{9}{16}$in long. Three lines should be drawn from C to D straight along the shaft and equal distances apart, as at E. One is known as the 'cock feather' and is usually a

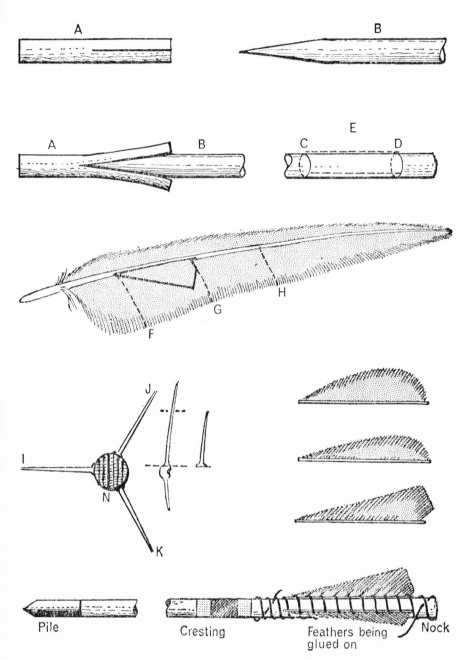

Fig 15 Bolt details: (*top*) splicing on a 'footing'; (*centre*) making the fletching; (*bottom*) gluing on the feathers. F, G and H, feather sections; I, J and K, feathers glued on to rear of bolt (N)

different colour from the other two. In shooting, this feather is placed down the groove.

The best feathers to use are stiff 'pinion' or main feathers from the wings of turkeys or geese. They can often be bought in stores or milliners' shops. There is a difference in the feathers of the right and left wings, so that the feather from one side only must be used on a bolt, for otherwise it will wobble in flight.

After you have cut through the quill at F, G and H (Fig 15), it is wise to soften the pieces by placing them between a folded cloth that you have wrung out in hot water. Then place a piece of feather flat on the edge of the bench, and using a flat piece of sheet steel or iron with a straight edge (eg a steel rule), place that on the vane and push the quill up flush to it. With a sharp knife pare off the quill level with the top surface of the metal plate. Still holding the feather down with the iron, shave off the surplus quill, leaving only a $\frac{1}{8}$in (3mm) strip as a foundation for the vane (Fig 15). To make sure that the feather will stand straight up on the shaft it is a good plan to grind the base by rubbing it on a piece of sandpaper placed flat on the bench. A spring paperclip is useful for holding the feather while you are doing this.

These pieces of feather are now stuck on the shaft 1in from the end (line D) and exactly along lines as described; Seccotine is the easiest glue to use. Rub a little on the base and allow it to become tacky before putting the feathers in position, then, having bound them with thread, as in the sketch, adjust them to the exact position, lying quite straight along the shaft, and leave to dry for twelve hours. When it is dry remove the thread and trim the feathers with sharp scissors or razor blade to the shape you prefer (some typical shapes are shown in Fig 15).

The quickest and most efficient way of trimming feathers to exactly the same shape is to use an electrically heated wire. The fletched bolt is placed in V slots cut in the sides of a box. An electric wire (eg part of an electric element) is then bent to the outline of the feather shape required. This cutting wire is so placed and wired up that when the bolt is turned in the slot each feather is cut to the chosen shape. The wire must be at a bright red heat; it may be necessary to wire a 2kW electric fire in series with it, or some other type of resistance.

It is usual to paint bolts with distinctive bands of colours just in front of the feathers. This is called the 'cresting', and in competitions each crossbowman should have his own colours so that his bolts can easily be distinguished in the target.

To prevent the glue of the feathers being affected by wet or damp it is a good plan to paint between the feathers as well, from the cresting to the back end, taking care not to get paint on the feathers.

THE TASSEL

Keep bolts clean: mud on them affects their flight. A tassel made of wool is usually hung on the belt and is used to wipe any bolts hitting the ground. Failing this you should keep a piece of rag in the pocket for this purpose.

THE QUIVER

Most crossbowmen, especially ladies, find it convenient to use a quiver to hold the bolts while shooting. Men can hold them in hip or trouser pockets, but they are usually not too conveniently placed as in a quiver.

A quiver can be made from a piece of pliable leather or other suitable material about 10in (25cm) long and 7in (18cm) wide. Holes can be punched along the sides and lower edge so that it can be drawn together into a tube with leather thongs, a circle of similar leather being sewn into the bottom. To complete the quiver sew to the top a leather loop with which it can be attached to the belt.

TARGETS AND BACKSTOPS

In the old days the most usual backstops for close shooting practice were simply mounds of earth (with any stones removed of course), with a sloping back and a fairly vertical front. When the grass grew over them they blended well into the rest of the field. They were called butts and were to be seen on most village greens in England. Sometimes they were built up of grass sods, which if carefully built were completely self-supporting. Provided there is a safe area behind the butt and it can be left permanently in place, this is a very satisfactory backstop for crossbow shooting.

Failing that the next cheapest method is to build up five or six bales of straw on a wooden platform, to keep them off the ground. To keep them steady stakes should be driven into the ground at either side, with a rope going over the top which can also hold down a piece of tarpaulin for protection against rain. If you use straw bales for crossbow shooting the shortness of the bolts makes it essential to fix some thick cardboard or similar material under the target face, to take the initial drive out of the bolt and prevent it burying itself in the bale.

As crossbow target faces in most competitive shooting are half the diameter of handbow targets it is possible to save expense when practising by providing two 2ft (60cm) diameter straw bosses sewn together, to make sure that there are no penetrations. If that is not possible a sheet or perhaps several sheets of cardboard should again be fixed behind the target face to take the punch out of the bolt. Speaking of cardboard reminds me that we have often used, both out of doors and indoors, packing cartons stuffed tight with newspaper and with a few layers of cloth inside the back, with the target face stuck on the front surface. The paper slows down the bolt and the cloth stops it going right through.

Target faces vary a great deal according to the rounds being shot and the distances required. They are usually printed on tough paper or cardboard but the long-lasting ones are on canvas. The target faces for field shooting can consist of black or white rings, animal silhouettes with rings or animals in full colour. The sizes and scoring for the different targets are listed with the shooting rules for the various rounds (see Appendix 2).

69

For indoor shooting, where there must be a large and adequate backstop, a special nylon netting has now been produced. (The source of supply is mentioned on page 36). Otherwise large sacks sewn edge to edge will make a curtain large enough to be thrown over a pole, so that there are two thicknesses of sacking in front, then the width of the pole gap and two thicknesses of sacking behind, usually make a satisfactory backstop. The air pocket in between the two lots of sacking helps to deaden stray bolts.

Page 71
(*right*) Modified Bakewell crossbow used by the Swedish team, with prod fixed above the bolt groove, and adjustable draw length

(*left*) The Swedish team: (*left to right*) G. Enström, Ingemar Edvinsson, Häkautantz and Dan Östtund

(*right*) Swedish indoor range

Page 72
(*left*) Cocking
with lever at the
Swiss Federal
Contest;
(*below*) The
shooting line at
the Swiss Federal
Contest

CHAPTER 4

Crossbows in Europe

As crossbows were used in warfare and hunting in most of the countries of Europe for several centuries it is only natural that there should be an instinctive interest in this weapon among many of the present-day descendants of the old crossbowmen. In Austria for example a group of farmers at Bad Aussee in the Salzkammargut area carry on this interest by making and shooting their own particular type of crossbow. Since winter is the season when they have time to spare they have built a 19¼yd (15m) indoor range and clubhouse on the farm. The targets are on timber backstops and have 1½in (3·8cm) diameter centres with zones counting 5, 4, 3, 2 and 1.

Protected by a timber screen one member stands near the targets, indicates the score and returns the bolts to the firing line by an endless rope device. Competition between neighbouring clubs is keen and on occasion there are special meetings at which the ladies take part in the shooting. Some of the prods in use are made of yew and most are cocked by hand, being for short range only.

Italy has clubs using the traditional long crossbows. These are about 6ft (1·88m) long and the front rests on a stand with the archer kneeling and holding the back of the stock on top of his shoulder. A team from one such club came over to England a few years ago for the 'Italian Week' in Liverpool. They brought their ancient bows with them and gave a demonstration of their shooting, wearing fifteenth-century dress for the occasion.

When the English team gave their demonstration with modern crossbows it was obvious that these were far superior to the medieval weapons.

Competitive crossbow shooting of very ancient origin is still carried on in Belgium today. It is called Popinjay shooting and was originally rather cruel. A live jay or pigeon would be tethered to a high steeple or mast and become the target for bowmen on the ground. But for many years now the live birds have been replaced by wooden substitutes stuck on spikes at the top of a 33yd (30m) pole. Normally there are three sizes of 'birds'. The largest (the 'cock') is placed at the very top of the pole; it is about 6in (15cm) long and has many feathers attached to it which allow it to float down when it is knocked off the perch. Lower down the pole on crossbars are two 'hens' which are smaller and have fewer feathers. Then there are two ducks and lower still perhaps twenty-four chickens, about 2in long with a little tuft of feathers. A considerable blow is needed to dislodge the birds from their spikes, so the bolts used have a special head made of horn and shaped quite flat in the front like a hammer.

Some towns have ancient clubs or 'fraternities' with their own grounds and clubhouses. In some public parks popinjay masts are set up where shooting can be practised. An entrance fee is charged and large numbers join in the competitions. Out of this considerable sum perhaps half is paid to the bowman who dislodges the cock. A lesser sum goes to those who hit the hens and an even smaller amount to those who hit the chickens. Participants wait for their turn and spectators stand under wire-netting to protect them from the falling bolts. In some parks there is an official whose job it is to retrieve the bolts and the birds if they fall wide. Strong and very wide-brimmed hats are also sometimes worn as protection. The high masts are counter-balanced so that they can be swung down to replace the birds that are knocked off. Some clubs have indoor ranges where the mast is held horizontally a short distance from the floor. The competition is carried on in the same way but against a back-stop and under cover.

Interest in the crossbow has spread slowly in Sweden but the growth has been steady and by degrees clubs are being formed in many parts of the country. The crossbows normally used are similar to modern English models but with certain modifications such as stirrups to aid cocking and adjustable stocks and butts (see page 71). The local rules do not restrict the target crossbows to 50lb (24kg) so considerably higher weights of prod are normally used, but they are all hand-cocked.

Field shooting is carried on under Swedish archery rules, which differ slightly from the FITA field rules in that the distance of the various targets is not known to the competitor but must be estimated, as in real hunting. Target competition both indoors and out of doors is run under the British and American shooting rules and Swedish clubs have competed in international mail matches against American and British teams, on one occasion making the top score.

It is little wonder that competitive shooting with the crossbow is a popular and growing sport in Switzerland. It was largely the crossbow in the hands of their ancestors that made it possible for them to throw off the tyranny of their Austrian overlords and form the Confederacy.

It is thought that the crossbow was introduced into Switzerland by the Swiss mercenaries serving under the Hohenstaufen emperors in the thirteenth century. The earliest evidence of this is on the seal and coat of arms of Johann von Hochdorf of Lucerne, which depict an early crossbow and date from 1235. When firearms improved and became more accurate they replaced crossbows as the main military weapon. However, the crossbow still held its interest for a great number of the Swiss, who continue to use it in the competitive target shooting that is still very popular in certain parts of the country.

Some of the equipment has of course been modified over the years. The original yew prod first gave way to one made of horn, sinew and wood, then to the iron prod and latterly to steel, with the present-day prod looking very much like the leaf of a car spring. The bowstring is now made of steel cable and the open sights have been replaced by much more sophisticated rifle sights.

The power of the prods used in this competitive shooting is about the same as that of the old war and hunting weapons, about 200lb (96kg) or more being a normal weight of pull. This means of course that the stock is built on quite robust lines (as can be seen in the accompanying illustrations on pages 72 and 80). Mechanical means of cocking the string are used, the most popular being the goat's-foot lever, which is of course removed before shooting.

Heavy steel-headed bolts are used. These are not fletched but are tapered somewhat at the back, leaving the head as the heaviest part so that the bolt will fly straight. The whole bolt weighs approximately 1oz (28gm). In practice the sights are adjusted for one particular bolt, so only that bolt is used with a given crossbow. This means that the bolt must be retrieved after every shot. The backstop behind the target face is made of thick wood and as the bolt has a screw thread at the front it is extracted by unscrewing with a spanner. This is a rather slow procedure but enables the shooting to be highly accurate. Young members of the family often help in retrieving the bolts and send them back by a small cable railway.

The normal distance shot in these competitions is 33yd (30m) and the targets used are approximately 5½in (14cm) in diameter with a ⅜in (98mm) black centre, 3¾in (9·25cm) area and a 5⁄16in (7mm) centre. The twenty rings count 1 to 20 (see Fig 16). The target faces are mounted on a 2in thick wooden base, which has a 3in diameter lead plug let into the centre so that when it is badly battered it can be taken out, hammered into shape and replaced in the wood.

On the ranges shooting is done from the kneeling position so that the bow hand can be supported with the elbow on the left knee. Because of the danger of the steel prod snapping, a thickly

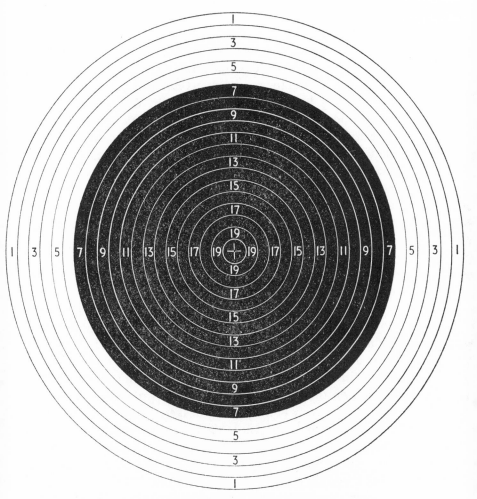

Fig 16   Swiss target face as used in Federal contests

padded glove is worn on the bow hand. Some prods are bound with adhesive tape as an additional precaution. The steel 'string' is securely fixed to the ends of the prod so that if the prod shatters the string will prevent it flying very far.

The Federal Tournament is held every five years and is a very popular occasion. It is run by the Federal Crossbow Association and there are many prizes in the form of badges, titles and so on. In addition the cantons and districts run their own competitions to find their local champion marksman. The rounds shot in competition for federal, canton, and club contests are five shots each for a five-man team, ten shots each for a club and thirty shots for the Federal Championship. The winner is dubbed the Crossbow King. At 33yd the shooting is very accurate and none of the competitors in the Federal Tournament would have much difficulty with the proverbial apple, though at a hundred paces it would no doubt be a different proposition. The towns where important contests are held arrange for official parades through the streets led by a band, followed by the town dignitaries and all the competitors with their standards and their crossbows carried on their shoulders.

In line with most of Europe during the Middle Ages the crossbow was widely used in the Netherlands in warfare and hunting. From the sixteenth century onwards a few societies in the South carried on the traditional form of crossbow shooting as a competitive sport. They used an unusual method of safety precaution on their shooting grounds—rows of tall baffle boards to catch any stray bolts. Fig 17 is a sketch made in 1544 of two shooting grounds in Amsterdam (recently published in the *Journal* of the Society of Archery Antiquaries) clearly showing these safety boards erected in both the archery and crossbow shooting grounds.

In addition to the few traditional societies in the South there is now a resurgence in the North, where several new clubs are carrying on the sport. The Netherlands Crossbow Federation now numbers sixty-nine clubs with a membership of 1,263.

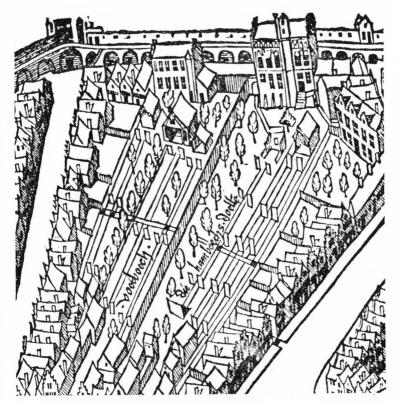

Fig 17 Amsterdam in 1544 showing five shooting lanes with upright baffle boards

Three distinct types of target shooting are carried on. At 33yd the heavy and strong Swiss type of crossbow (often made in Switzerland) is used. The bolts and targets are similar to their Swiss counterparts, the bolts having the screw thread on the front, so that they can be screwed out of the lead target centre (see Fig 18). These crossbows and shooting methods are used by the teams chosen to represent the Netherlands in international competitions such as the European Championships.

In local competitions other distances are habitually shot with

79

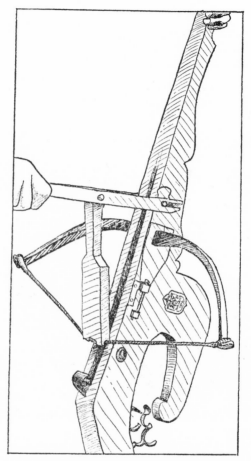

Fig 18   Swiss-made crossbow used in the Netherlands
with steel prod and wooden lever

a particular type of crossbow for the distance. In the South
11yd (10m) shooting is more popular, whereas in the North,
East and West the 22yd (20m) style is preferred. The safety
catch boards are used for all distances. In these tournaments the
crossbowmen shoot in groups of six according to the scores
made in previous tournaments. For example: in the Honour

Division are those who have made 91 points or over; in the A Division those with 87 to 90 points; in the B Division those with 85 to 86 points; C Division those below 85 points.

Crossbows had an important place in German warfare and sport for many years. A particular type of popinjay shooting attracted great numbers of participants in the larger towns, especially in Dresden. Rather than several imitation 'birds' as used in other parts of Europe, the target shot at in Dresden and elsewhere in Germany was a large single 'bird' built up of flat pieces of wood shaped like feathers and loosely fixed to form wings, leg, neck and head (see Fig 19). Each part of the 'bird'

Fig 19   The Dresden 'bird'

knocked down counted a certain score and won a prize of a definite value.

Special blunt bolts were used, of course, but spectators were well advised to stand under specially constructed shelters with wire netting roofs while watching any form of popinjay shooting. Bolts and pieces of the 'bird' when falling from a height can give a nasty knock.

CHAPTER 5

Crossbows in the United States

Crossbow archers form a welcome section of the National Archery Association and come under the overall administration of that body. There is however a President of National Crossbowmen, with a Vice-President and a Secretary/Treasurer. An annual business meeting is held to elect officers, pass accounts and discuss any matters affecting crossbow shooting. As they have such close links with longbowmen, crossbowmen are able to participate in most of the longbow national competitions, although they shoot on their own targets at the various distances.

The National Crossbow Championships are shot at the same place and concurrently with the National Archery Championships, usually in early August. The championships are decided on four American rounds, shot on different days. A single American round as shot by both the longbowmen and the crossbowmen consists of thirty bolts (or arrows) shot at 60yd, 50yd and 40yd (55m, 45·75m and 36·6m). It has always been traditional to shoot the longer distances first, presumably because in warfare the enemy gradually approached the archers!

The ninety bolts of the American round are all shot by crossbowmen on 2ft (60cm) diameter targets (half the diameter of the longbow targets). These targets have the five rings of the normal English targets; counting from the centre gold (yellow) 9, red 7, blue 5, black 3, white 1.

During the five days of the annual NAA Tournament the crossbowmen also shoot an international crossbow round. This consists of thirty bolts shot at 71yd, 54·7yd and 38·3yd (65m,

50m, 35m) on the 32in (80cm) FITA (Fédération Internationale de Tir-à-l'Arc) target face. A clout shoot is also contested at 148yd (135m) on special targets marked on the ground. This can be shot both ways if there are two safe ends.

At the end of the four 'championship American rounds' the three highest scoring men and women participate in what is known as the King's and Queen's Round (see Tournament Rules on page 125).

In addition to competition in the national and state tournament an increasing number of indoor professional archery ranges all over the United States are making provision for crossbow shooting alongside the longbow lanes.

For the last four years the NAA have arranged an indoor championship which is decided on what is called the 900 American round: 30 bolts at 60yd, 50yd and 40yd (55m, 47·75m and 36·6m), but on a ten-ring target making, a score of 900 possible.

What is known as the Winter League Tournament is also run by the NAA each year; recently crossbowmen have been taking part in their own section. The special round shot is called the 300 round and consists of 96 bolts shot at 20yd (18·28m) on a 10in (25·4cm) black and white target with five rings counting 5, 4, 3, 2, 1. There are six bolts per end.

Many states now organise crossbow hunting for big game as well as game birds at certain seasons. As crossbows are easier to shoot accurately than the composite longbows and can be used either kneeling or prone behind cover, they must be a more humane weapon for hunting. They are less likely to maim without killing and, being much quieter than firearms, are not likely to disturb game very far around. It is therefore likely that more and more hunting will be done with crossbows as their effectiveness is better understood by the authorities. In addition to the states that allow crossbow hunting at certain seasons there are private ranches offering crossbow hunting for big game such as elk, deer, bear and so on.

Many of the longbow enthusiasts who hunt in the winter practice on field archery courses during the summer. It is therefore likely that crossbowmen who are interested in hunting will also swell the great numbers who go in for field shooting. One side of the sport in which Americans have particularly excelled recently is crossbow flight shooting. The object of flight shooting is to achieve the greatest possible distance regardless of a target. It entails the use of specially designed crossbows and bolts, one of the great difficulties being finding suitable fields in which to get sufficient distance of clear space. A glance at the following report will emphasise this problem. Writing from San Francisco to Fred Isles, the President of the National Crossbowmen, George Ahavekin wrote in 1968:

I was able to attend the California State Flight Shoot as an observer for one day only. I flew in and witnessed the shooting on Saturday morning. However it was not until the next day, Sunday, that Harry Drake shooting the last of his six arrows (bolts) achieved the present official record of 1,429 yards . . . Since Ivanpah Dry Lake, while excellent for longbow flight shooting wherein longer arrows are involved, is not equally suitable for smaller crossbow arrows (bolts) which are hard to find, I spent the next couple of days looking for a better site for the latter type of shooting. Good fortune finally guided me to a site which I hope will eventually be selected for conducting the crossbow flight event. More about this place hereafter. There was time to lay out a line of stakes 100 yards apart for a sufficient distance in the direction of the prevailing wind of that particular afternoon.

Out of eight shots, I had three over 1,400 yards the best of which was 1,495. I became aware that some modifications were necessary, so I went home and spent two days on the problem. On Saturday afternoon I was back on the site. Using three different crossbows I got off eight shots before the sun got too low in the sky. I found seven arrows that evening and the eighth on the following morning. Here are the distances in order of shooting attained October 12th 1968. Bow No. 1: 1,302, 1,475 and 1,506 yards (right after shooting 1,475 arrow I made an adjustment that may have been important). Bow No. 2: 1,554, 1,445 and 1,590 yards. Bow No. 3: 1,562, 1,615.

An average distance for these eight arrows was approximately 1,506 yards. On a day previous to the California State Flight Shoot in June 1968 Harry Drake achieved his best unofficial mark, 1,480.

Several factors enter into the attainment of these very long distances: the special design and speed of the bow itself, the shape and weight of the bolt and the angle at which the shot is made (43° from the horizontal should give the maximum distance possible with any given bow, according to the mathematicians). Another important factor is the amount of dust and moisture in the air. I am not aware of distances greater than the above achieved with a crossbow, but even these records may not stand for long.

CHAPTER 6

History of the Crossbow

It is natural to assume that the simple one-piece bow was invented first and that in the course of time a more mechanical method of aiming and release was developed when a short strong bow was fitted to a stock and the string was released by a form of trigger. It would thus have been easier to control and more accurate. This sequence of events is supported by all the evidence we have to date. It is probably more truthful to say that the first handbow was discovered rather than invented, for it is quite feasible to imagine an early Stone Age man discovering to his surprise that a sapling with a sinew line tied to the top and bottom would throw his spear farther than he could throw it by hand.

However that may be it is a fact that the use of the first simple bow is shrouded in the mists of antiquity. Whereas there is no evidence of the crossbow being in use before about 1050 BC it appears that large siege engines were used by some of the armies early in the period of the Warring States of China. These worked according to various mechanical principles, all with the object of casting large stones or heavy javelins at or over the besieged walls. As very often happens with a successful invention that has first been made large and crude but eventually becomes better designed, smaller in size and weight and even portable, this is very likely what may have happened with these war machines in China, and the earliest we hear of the use of portable crossbows comes when the Mongol Chou people from the steppes attacked the Shang State in 1050 BC by advancing along the Yellow River Valley in chariots and armed with crossbows. Later, during the Han dynasty (206 BC–AD 200) crossbows were evidently quite widely used, as many examples of these Han weapons still exist. Japanese archaeologists unearthed a stock and trigger mechanism of this type (thought to have been made in about AD 150) in Korea (see Fig 20). Another stock, trigger mechanism and two prods were found in the diggings at Constant Virtue Hill, Ch'ang-sha, Hunan, China. Being made of a good alloy of

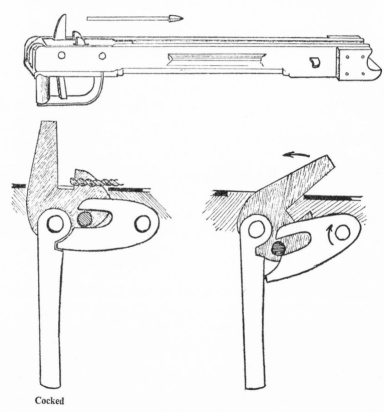

Cocked

Fig 20   Ancient Chinese crossbow and lock from 300 BC to c AD 200

Page 89 Carol Pelosi of Greenbelt, Maryland, the American Woman Champion
and record holder of 1973

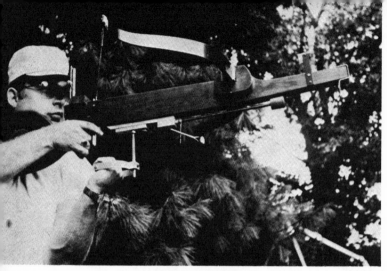

Page 90
(*left*) Thomas Hock of Cincinnati, the American champion of 1974

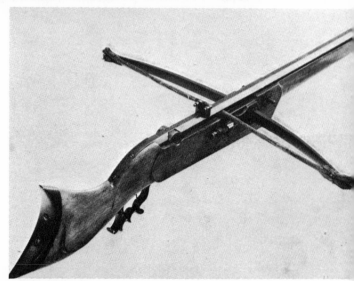

(*right*) Belgian bullet crossbow with side pegs for the 'goat's-foot lever'

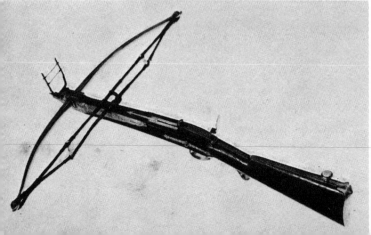

(*left*) English bullet crossbow (nineteenth century) with built-in lever

bronze and tin the trigger mechanisms of the Han period were very durable and many can still be seen today.

Claims to have 'invented' the siege engine have been put forward at later dates and in countries other than China. For instance the Bible refers to King Uzziah in 2 Chronicles, Chapter 26 in these terms: 'And he made in Jerusalem engines invented by cunning men, to be on the towers and upon the bulwarks, to shoot arrows and great stones withal.' Most authorities put the date of King Uzziah as around 600 BC, long after the Warring States of China. Then there was Heron of Alexandria (284–221 BC) who wrote about siege engines that may very well have included methods of construction similar to that used for a crossbow. Later, in 214 BC, when the Roman general Marcellus attacked Syracuse, Archimedes, who was living in Syracuse at the time, directed the use of large war engines that he had invented and constructed. The besieging Romans had evidently not expected them and for a long time they were prevented from overcoming the town. It is clear that these machines projected large stones and heavy javelins over quite a distance creating havoc and terror among the enemy. For two years Syracuse held off the Romans, but eventually the town was overcome by a blockade; Archimedes himself was killed in the final surprise attack in 212 BC.

A little later than this in about 150 BC a man of Byzantium called Philon designed a quick-firing *ballista* in which as one bolt was fired another dropped into its place ready to be fired as fast as the cable could be recocked.

By now the Roman generals appreciated the effectiveness of these various war engines and so we read of their use by Vespasian against the town of Jotapata in AD 67; by Hadrian against Jerusalem in AD 70, and by Julius Caesar in his wars. All these were large machines dragged into position by teams of horses or men and used chiefly for siege work, but many of them were constructed on mechanical principles that were afterwards used in very much smaller portable editions.

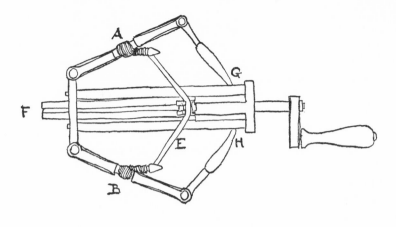

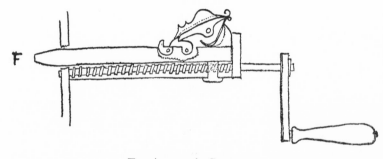

THE ASSASSIN'S CROSSBOW

Fig 21 Remarkable fifteenth-century crossbow (of which it is thought there are very few examples in existence) in the Birmingham Museum. It is very small, only about 10in long, and has no wide prod, but works on the same principle as some of the huge war engines used in Roman times. The propelling force is developed by twisting skeins of sinew.

A square steel framework at A and B allows skeins of sinew to be twisted up so that the bowstring E is pulled taut. The bolt groove F, with the latch and trigger attached, is wound forward until the string is caught in the latch and then wound back again forcibly tightening the twist in the skeins. The bolt is placed in the groove against the string, the weapon pointed at the quarry and the trigger pressed down by the thumb. The two tapered supports at G and H fit loosely into holes at the side of the 'stock' so that when the string is released they can be pulled out of the holes and the whole weapon collapsed quite flat and concealed in a pocket or under a cloak. It is obvious that the object of this construction was concealment. With the right kind of bolt this 'assassin's' crossbow would have been as effective as a pistol but a whole lot quieter and almost as easily hidden.

Writing on archery in the Roman world, David Hill, MA, of the Royal Toxophilite Society expresses the opinion that there is good evidence to suggest that crossbows were often used against the Roman legions. As confirmation of this he quotes two contemporary historians as stating that at the siege of Syracuse both archers and users of 'scorpions' shot through small loop-holes in the walls at the Roman attackers. The fact that these loop-holes were too small to allow the normal large *ballista* to be used and that a later historian stated that what were formerly called scorpions were subsequently known as *manuballistae*, which killed with small darts, seems to make it fairly certain that hand-held crossbows were used in that siege. There is also a later report that 'about sixty large and small scorpions' were captured in New Carthage by Scipio Africanus. David Hill also reports on the existence in le Puy, France, of two sculptures of presumed Roman origin depicting hunters carrying crossbows, while in a Romano-British grave at Burbage in Wiltshire the 'nut' or catch of a crossbow has been found.

Some historians have expressed the opinion that while bows as well as crossbows were widely used during the Roman Empire, reports of the battles and warfare in general seldom mention their use because they were so familiar and therefore taken for granted.

If, as seems evident, the Romans came in contact with the crossbow at Syracuse in 214 BC and subsequently made use of this effective weapon themselves under the name of scorpions and later of *manuballistae*, this gives some weight to the often stated opinion that it was the Italian states that first introduced the crossbow to Europe. The alternative name by which it was known tends to confirm this. In Italian it was commonly called an *arbalest* from the Latin *arcus*, bow, and *ballista*, a Roman war machine.

However, we are still left with the question of whether Archimedes did independently re-invent these hand-held *ballistae* for the protection of Syracuse or whether he heard of or actually saw an example from China, where they had been in use for many years. Although the Romans had not themselves contacted China, except for a few traders who reached it by sea, the Persians (who were great archers) had contact with China during the time of the Han dynasty. It is certainly difficult to believe that they never came across or took an interest in the Han crossbow, which was so much in evidence at that time. Since the Romans had a good deal of contact with the Persians, albeit in warfare, it is possible that they got to know about crossbows from the Persians independently of Archimedes. While there is not much evidence of crossbows being used in England before the Norman Conquest, it is likely that individual Roman legionaries brought them with them when they occupied Britain (see page 91).

Most of the early European crossbows were powered by prods of some pliable wood such as yew or ash, but those made in Asia may well have been of composite construction like the Mongolian, Chinese and Indian handbows, only shorter. The construction of composite bows and prods in those days was such a highly skilled and difficult process that we do not hear of any European or English bowyers mastering the art. The materials took months to prepare. The buffalo horn had to be imported, presumably from Asia, while the sinew from the heel of bullocks had to soak for weeks and then be shredded out to silk-like threads. The well-seasoned wood core had to be carefully shaped and the whole glued together with a specially prepared glue obtained in some cases from sturgeon (now called isinglass).

As armour improved there was a need for stronger crossbows to be effective against it. With the growing understanding of the tempering of metals powerful steel crossbows came to be used in the eleventh century and the Crusading armies found that they provided the answer to some of their problems against the mounted archers of the East.

Strangely enough crossbows do not appear to be illustrated on the Bayeux tapestry, perhaps because of the current Pope's interdict (see page 98). But there is evidence to suggest that some were in use among William I's invading forces at Hastings. In a report of the battle by Guy of Amiens, Duke William is said to have had the support of *ballistantes*, which evidently meant crossbowmen. There is also strong evidence that his son, William Rufus, was killed by a bolt from a hunting crossbow in the New Forest in Hampshire. And the Domesday Book, compiled in 1086, mentions one 'Odo the Arbalaster', though it is not known whether he made crossbows or shot them— perhaps both.

As we have mentioned, the Crusaders made good use of this weapon against the Saracens. They sometimes employed un- usual methods to gain the same end, which evidently horrified Princess Anna Comnena of Constantinople. She was the daughter of the Emperor Alexius I and in about 1120 wrote in her *Alexiad*:

> This crossbow is a bow of the barbarians, quite unknown to the Greeks; and it is not stretched by the right hand pulling the string whilst the left pulls the bow in a contrary direction, but he who stretches this warlike and very far-shooting weapon must lie, one might say, almost on his back and apply both feet strongly against the semi-circle of the bow and with his two hands pull the string with all his might in the contrary direction. In the middle of the string is a socket, a cylindrical kind of cup fitted to the string itself, and about as long as an arrow of considerable size which reaches from the string to the very middle of the bow, and through this arrows of many sorts are shot out. The arrows used with this bow are very short in length, but very thick, fitted in front with a heavy iron tip. And in discharging them the string shoots them out with enormous violence and force, and whatever these darts chance to hit, they do not fall back, but they pierce through the shield, then cut through a heavy iron corslet and wing their way through and out the other side.

There is no doubt that crossbows were used very effectively by some of the Crusaders. In 1191, during the Third Crusade, Richard Coeur-de-Lion gained a resounding victory at the Battle of Arsuf against Saladin's forces, chiefly by the use of crossbows in the hands of the Crusaders.

95

Later the Genoese mercenaries adopted the crossbow as their chief weapon and used it with great effect in the service of many different armies. For them it had several advantages. The ammunition was cheaper and less bulky than arrows. It was better suited for shooting from behind a shield or any other kind of cover and was more accurate and effective in the hands of less skilled soldiers. The one thing against it was the time it took to reload and shoot. The fact that it was often less effective in battle than the English longbow may be accounted for by three factors: first the more rapid 'fire' of the English longbow, secondly the better discipline of the English bowmen and thirdly the poor generalship and lack of control of the opposing cavalry. When the Genoese crossbow mercenaries appeared to let down the French knights so badly, at the Battle of Crécy in 1346, the excuse they made was that the heavy and continuous rain made their crossbow strings useless. Now if, like the longbowmen, their strings had been made of Flemish hemp (or linen) we would agree with the English archers and subsequent historians that that was a very lame excuse, because wet weather makes a hemp bowstring even stronger. But suppose their crossbow strings were made of sinew, the strongest known fibre at that time? Being soaked with rain their bowstrings would certainly become useless, for under tension wet sinew stretches and stretches. I have myself, incidentally, seen several old crossbows strung with sinew strings.

If legend is any guide the crossbow was in wide use in Switzerland by the twelfth century. Like Robin Hood of England the name of William Tell of Switzerland is known to everyone, yet no one can be quite sure that either of these famous peasants really existed. Although some of their deeds have gained somewhat in the telling I am convinced that both men were real personalities.

The main story of William Tell describes him as a proud peasant living at Burglen, a village in the canton of Uri, in 1291. The Austrian Hapsburgs had subjugated the Swiss and to humiliate the peasantry some of the Austrian bailiffs placed their hats on poles in the centre of the towns and required the Swiss to bow to them as they passed. This was too much for William Tell who refused to comply when he visited Altdorf, near Lake Lucerne, with his young son. He was well known as an expert marksman with the crossbow, so when he was brought before Herr Gessler the tyrannical bailiff, this fact suggested a cruel test to Gessler. If William Tell could split an apple placed on the head of his young son, Tell's life would be spared. Some say that one hundred paces was the required range but distances become so exaggerated in the retelling of these shooting stories that it was likely to have been very much less.

However William Tell took up the challenge, which in itself suggests that he did not consider the feat impossible. He also declared that he carried another bolt in his belt which was reserved for Gessler himself. Having hit the apple without injuring his son, the story goes that he was later being taken to prison by boat when a severe storm arose on Lake Lucerne. This storm blew them badly off course and being an expert helmsman he was given the task of trying to get them to their intended destination. Instead, he took the opportunity to steer the boat near enough to land to jump ashore and escape into the mountains which he knew so well. A little later he fulfilled his threat and killed Gessler from an ambush in 'Hohle Gasse' or 'The Hollow Way' near Kussnocht, not far from Lucerne. It is said it was this act which became the signal for the Swiss peasants to rise and throw off the Austrian overlords.

Whether these details of William Tell's story are accurate or not it is still true that about that time the three clans in the district, Schwyz (from which Switzerland gets its name), Uri and Unterwald united in a Confederation and took the 'Oath of Eternal Alliance' which might be called the Swiss 'Declaration of Independence'. One translation reads:

In the name of God, Amen. We the people of Uri, Schwyz and Unterwalden, considering the evil times that are upon us and the better

97

to protect and defend ourselves, swear upon oath to aid and succour one another mutually with our deeds and counsel, with our strong right arms and earthly goods, with all our might and soul, against each and all who do us hurt and wrong.

With one voice do we swear and promise not to tolerate in our valleys the dominion of foreign judges.

None of us shall do harm unto a comrade whether to his body or to his possessions. He amongst us who shall be judged blameworthy shall repair his wrong doing. Should discord arise between Confederates, then shall our elders forgather and act as mediators.

This our covenant, is drawn up for the good of all and shall with God's help endure for ever.

Delivered in the year of Our Lord 1291 in the beginning of the month of August.

Again, even if Friedrich Schiller in telling so graphically the story of William Tell, drew not only from local legends but also a little from his own imagination, we will be ever grateful to him for providing Rossini with the material for his opera on the subject, especially his well known overture including the storm on the Lake.

Not only in Italy and Switzerland but also in France and Spain the popularity of the crossbow grew, until in the thirteenth century the rank of Master of the Crossbowmen was held in high esteem. In fact in Spain an élite Corps of Crossbowmen was formed among men of high birth. Its members became very famous for their striking uniform and equipment.

In England the crossbow had been discouraged by the authorities for a period, partly because, as we have seen, in 1139 the Pope's Lateran Council placed a ban on the use of crossbows in warfare, except against infidels, and partly because the English longbowmen had become so proficient and effective by constant practice that it was thought unwise to allow another weapon to distract their attention and divide their interest. When Richard I came back from the Crusades, however, he reintroduced them. The fact that he himself was killed by a crossbow bolt while besieging Chalus Castle was seen by some as retribution for defying the Pope's ban.

There are many indications that crossbows were growing

more popular, if not in the English armies at least in the hunting field, where rate of fire was not so important. It is interesting to note that several estates in England were held in return for the service of delivering a crossbow and the thread for the string when the King passed through them.

No one who has travelled on the Continent of Europe, especially if he has come into contact with the many archery fraternities, can have failed to see the very many paintings of the martyrdom of St Sebastian, who is looked upon as the patron

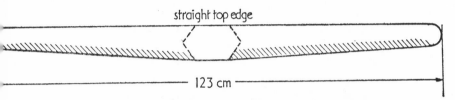

straight top edge

123 cm

THE BERKHAMPSTEAD PROD

Fig 22 Yew crossbow prod found in a remarkable state of preservation in the muddy silt at the bottom of the inner moat at Berkhampstead Castle, where it is thought to have been for about six hundred years. It is now in the British Museum.

At first it was thought to be a short Saxon handbow, being only 49in (1·23m) long, but after a full and careful examination by Robert C. Brown of the Society of Archer Antiquaries (see vol 10 of their 1967 journal) it was proved beyond doubt to be the one-piece yew prod of a strong crossbow.

The two main reasons for making this claim are the fact that the dimensions of the limbs would mean a draw weight of at least 150lb (64kg), much stronger than could be used for a handbow, and the fact that one edge of the limbs is straight along the full length of the bow, making it suitable to be fitted into a crossbow stock but not suitable to be hand held.

In any case yew wood was the normal material at that time for crossbow prods and one as strong as that would need to be cocked by a goat's-foot lever or cranquin.

saint of all archers, both longbowmen or crossbowmen. He is usually depicted shot through by crossbow bolts—perhaps an indication of the popularity of the crossbow in the Middle Ages. Legend has it that he was born at Narbonne in AD 255 and went to Rome to enter the army, eventually becoming a captain in the Praetorian Guard (the Imperial Bodyguard). When it was discovered that he had become a Christian, Diocletian ordered him to be executed by archers. This order was carried out and he was left for dead, but a Christian lady named Irene tended his wounds and he recovered. Later he had the temerity to upbraid the Emperor who as a result had him beaten to death with clubs. This time another Christian lady named Faustina found his body and buried him in the catacombs in AD 288. Subsequently the Basilica of St Sebastian was built in 367 near the place of his burial and many artists and sculptors sought to immortalise the event. One such famous picture is in the National Gallery in London, entitled 'The martyrdom of St Sebastian AD 288' painted by Antonio Pollainolo in 1475. In 826 his remains were removed to Soissons, France.

It is recorded that after the destruction of the Spanish Armada certain noblemen of Queen Elizabeth's court, fearing that the King of Spain might seek revenge by making an attempt on the life of the Queen formed themselves into a bodyguard for the protection of her person. They were known as the 'Companie of Leige Bowmen of the Queene' and many privileges were conferred upon them. When a new and improved type of crossbow was produced by a Dutchman named Vander Foheman the 'Companie' tested them out and adopted them as an additional weapon. It is also known that the Queen herself enjoyed hunting on horseback with the crossbow.

Those who have hunted with the normal crossbow using the 10 or 12in (25 or 30cm) bolt must have been faced with the difficulty of finding the bolts that have missed the quarry and buried themselves in the undergrowth or grass. How often does the huntsman resolve to watch where his bolt lands if it should miss but how seldom does he keep his resolve when the quarry jumps and runs to cover, followed of course by the eye of the disappointed hunter? It is then that one wishes for bolts that cost nothing, or so little that they can be ignored. No doubt such wishes resulted in the great popularity of stone bows and bullet bows in the seventeenth, eighteenth and nineteenth centuries in England and on the Continent of Europe.

The arquebus and musket were taking the place of crossbows in warfare but in hunting, especially for larger animals, the accuracy and comparative silence of the crossbow were an advantage. For smaller animals and birds, however, a crossbow shooting small stones or bullets was a definite saving on ammunition yet gave a strong enough blow to stun or kill.

The early stone bows made in Europe and also in parts of Asia had a characteristic curved stock between the latch and the front sight. This gave free flight to the string and the small pouch holding the stone, without any friction on a bolt groove. Another great difference from the normal crossbow was the construction of the string. In order to hold the pouch with the front wide open for the stone to fly out there had to be a double string with spreaders keeping the two portions apart, with the pouch fixed between them.

Most of the early stone bows were fitted with steel prods but were not very powerful and were cocked by hand. But as time went on competition with the musket caused the prods to be made stronger and the goat's-foot lever had to be employed (see page 28). But the skill and ingenuity of the craftsmen making crossbows soon led to the lever being let into a channel in the stock with the catch fixed to the front end of the lever. This was much more convenient than having to detach the lever after cocking the string and then stowing it away. You merely brought the lever up and forward so that the hook caught the string, then pulling the lever back and down into the channel cocked the string ready to shoot (see page 29).

Unless a stone is perfectly round it cannot be expected to fly true, so the next improvement was the bullet-shooting crossbow. For this, lead bullets were made of uniform weight and size. In some cases the stock was open (see English bullet crossbow on page 90), but in others there was a slight groove covered over to form a type of barrel (see Belgian bullet crossbow on page 90). For many years stone bows and bullet bows were very popular in England for shooting vermin, small game and birds. With the increased demand for good weapons we find several centres becoming well known for the excellent crossbows made by good craftsmen in the area. This was true of several towns in Lancashire, and Warrington in particular was noted for its steel prods. By this time, about 1850, muskets were becoming more reliable and accurate so that the use of crossbows for hunting began to wane.

Handbows of varying craftsmanship have, of course, been used for thousands of years by the natives of almost every country, but in 1929 Major Powell-Cotton found tribes in the Southern Cameroons who used crossbows with the same method of releasing the string as did the Chinese in their repeating cross-bows years before. In the magazine *Man* he reported that 'practically every tribesman was armed with them'. This is the first known example of comparatively primitive peoples dis-covering how to make and use crossbows. In both cases the drawn string was held in a notch cut in the stock with a small hole going through the stock immediately below it. To release the string a small rod was forced up through the hole and thus pushed the string out of the notch.

In the case of the African tribesmen the stock consists of a long wooden pole split to within a few inches of the prod. This split is held open by a plug of wood while the string is pulled back into the notch and the poisoned bolt fixed in place against the string. When a quarry is found the plug is pulled out of the split, aim is taken and the two pieces of the split stock are squeezed together, thus pushing the rod up through the hole and the string out of the notch (see Fig 23). Although they do not appear to be very powerful bows they were evidently quite effective in obtaining food and for dealing with enemies; the use of a poison obtained from a local plant probably helped.

Fig 23   Crossbow used by West African tribesmen

Before we leave the historical and warlike story of the cross-bow and to help readers to get some idea of the power and effectiveness of these weapons I should like to quote Sir Ralph Payne-Gallway in his standard work *The Crossbow*, published in 1906.

I was fortunate in obtaining from Nuremberg a fine example of one of these large weapons . . . The steel bow is, however, the original one and of as good temper as ever, though it was made in Genoa over four hundred years ago.

The bow [prod] is 3ft. 2in. long and at its centre 2½in. wide and 1in. thick.

Shooting this crossbow from the shoulder, with a bolt 3oz. in weight and 14in. in length, I have attained a range of 460 yards, and at 60 yards I have sent a bolt right through a deal plank ¾in. thick.

By suspending the crossbow in a perpendicular position from a beam, and then attaching heavy weights to a rope fastened to the centre of its bowstring, I was able to determine its strength of pull. The total weight required to draw the string of its bow 7in., or from a state of rest to the catch of the lock, is 1,200lbs. or over half a ton! . . . Not withstanding its immense strength of pull, by the aid of its portable little fifteenth-century windlass, the string of this crossbow can be stretched to the catch of its lock by the fingers of one hand, showing the great power and cleverly designed efficiency of the windlass of a mediaeval crossbow.

It is perhaps, worth recording here, that in the autumn of 1901, I shot several bolts with this weapon across the Menai Straits, from the battery of Fort Belan to Abermenai Point; this was done in the presence of a number of sporting friends who were interested in the attempt, and who declared that the feat was impossible.

The distance achieved by the bolts, according to Ordnance Survey, was between 440 and 450 yards.

It is most unlikely that a missile of any kind has previously been projected without the aid of gunpowder, from one shore to the other, across this arm of the sea.

Sir Ralph also mentions that the weight, in the hand, of this crossbow was about 18lb (8·16kg), but that most battle cross-

103

bows known to him weighed about 15 to 16lb (6·80 to 7·25kg), with prods of 2ft 7in or 2ft 8in (78cm or 80cm).

In contrast to the former use of crossbows in hunting and warfare the weapon is now being used increasingly to protect animal life. In recent years veterinary scientists have felt the need to capture wild animals in order to mark them or examine them for disease. Originally the method used was to trap them or chase them to exhaustion in Land Rovers and then lassoo them. Such methods proved very time-wasting and expensive, apart from often being fatal for the animal.

With the production of tranquillising drugs, however, the need was for a satisfactory method of delivering the required dose into the animal's bloodstream. Firearms and powerful air rifles have been used to shoot a small hypodermic syringe which carries the drug and releases it on penetrating the animal's skin. One disadvantage of this method is the loud report made by these weapons and the consequent frightening off of all animals in a wide area. Another disadvantage is the high cost of hypodermic darts suitable for use in these weapons. In consequence of this Dr Short of the Cambridge University Veterinary College approached one of the leading makers of crossbows in England to collaborate in producing a crossbow capable of shooting a tubular bolt carrying a drug. One problem was how to release the dose of the drug after the hypodermic needle had pierced the hide of the animal and not before. After considerable experimentation it was found that the easiest method was to close the front of the sharp needle with a tight polythene cap, which was cut through as the needle pierced the hide. It was also essential to pump the drug into the bloodstream with some force. This was eventually done by fitting a plunger and car-type valve at the back of the tube and introducing air pressure from a pump or CO_2 pressure from a Sparklet bulb behind the drug (see page 108).

Most of the drugs used are on the dangerous list and not freely available; it is therefore usual for a veterinary surgeon to prescribe the type of drug and the dosage according to the kind of animal and its size. Drugs are now available for most animals and if they can be approached to within 50yd or so the crossbow is quite effective.

Among the semi-wild animals park deer are usually the easiest to capture in this way, even on foot. Herds of wild animals can usually be approached to within a reasonable distance (say 40yd or 50yd) in a Land Rover and individual animals 'darted' from the cab without the rest of the herd being disturbed. This method is used very extensively in setting up national game parks and is also found useful for transferring animals to safe regions when the building of dams causes flooding of large areas.

All the usual rules for stalking wild animals must be followed if you are to get within the necessary distance for an effective tranquillising shot: clothing and weapons must be of a colour that blends into the surroundings; the wind must be blowing from the animal to the stalker; movements must be slow and noiseless and you must 'freeze' if the quarry looks straight at you. If it is possible to take up a position where the animal is likely to wander towards you, you can then keep your sights trained on the animal until it is near enough for an effective shot. This raises one problem, however. A tranquillising dart must not hit a bone but most be placed in a fleshy part of the body. An animal slowly approaching with its head down, perhaps feeding, offers its shoulders for an accurate shot. Great care must be taken not to hit the spine, however. If on the other hand the head is raised the two upper legs offer the best target, though in this case the safe areas are not large and the head must be carefully avoided.

If the animal is likely to pass within effective range on either side it is best to wait until it is nearly broadside so that you can place the dart in the rump. Provided that the animal is not startled by movement, sight or scent you can even allow it to pass, thus presenting the whole of its rump for an effective shot.

105

In this method of getting within range it is best to kneel on the right knee (for a right-handed shooter) and if possible behind a tree or shrub of some sort. (Watch out that the limb of the bow is not going to hit the trunk of the tree when you loose the dart.) As most animals, especially grazers, seldom look up into trees it is often a help to construct a hide in one of the trees within range of the animal's habitual track to a water hole, salt lick or even a wallow. The earlier you do this before the shoot the better.

The time it takes an animal to go down after receiving a tranquillising dart depends to a great extent on the skill of the veterinary surgeon in judging the weight of the animal and choosing the drug and quantity to use. Somewhere between four and twenty minutes is usual. After hitting the animal you should remain in cover and keep still and quiet. In this case your quarry is not likely to move far and after a slight jump may even go on feeding until it gets unsteady on its legs and eventually rolls over. Even then, approach with care if it is a dangerous animal. One vet I know when dealing with a very wild lioness only recently out of the jungle, insisted on her front and back paws being roped together before he would approach her with his instruments; although she was fast asleep under the drug, perhaps he was right.

Page 107 The author loading a hypodermic dart on the Yeoman crossbow

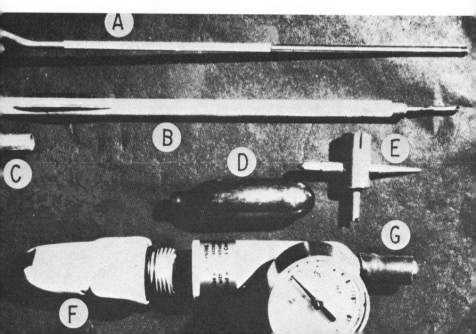

Page 108 (*above*) Type of English modern crossbow used for tranquillising deer and other animals (note the wood and fibreglass prod); (*below*) animal tranquillising equipment: A graduated rod and handle for drawing the drug up into the dart; B feathered hypodermic dart with barbed needle; C cap at rear of the dart; D CO_2 cylinder; E Schrader valve tool; F 'Sparklet' pressuriser with gauge; G connector to back of the dart

APPENDIX 1

The British Crossbow Society: Rules of Shooting

1 Crossbowmen do not compete with longbowmen. They compete with and against each other for awards within their own division.

2 Targets are one half the size specified for longbows for the same round, except for the Clout, Big Game and Field Rounds where the same target is used. The target is 24in diameter; the centre circle is $4\frac{4}{5}$in with a white centre $2\frac{2}{5}$in and a black band $1\frac{3}{16}$in. The centre circle is ringed by four concentric bands $2\frac{2}{5}$in wide. Scoring is 9, 7, 5, 3, 1.

3 Rules are the same as for longbowmen except where they conflict with the rules given in this section.

4 The Crossbow Field Captain is specially appointed to supervise the crossbowmen. His duties and authority correspond to those of the Field Captain of longbowmen, his decision being final, unless appeal is made to the British Crossbow Society.

5 The crossbow and parts may be made of any material.

6 Crossbows shall be drawn by hand. No mechanical aids for drawing shall be permitted.

7 Shooting: crossbowmen shall stand to shoot and shall shoot offhand. No rest of any description shall be permitted.

8 Assignment to targets: two crossbowmen shall be assigned

per target. Two targets per 4ft boss on target shoots only.

9   Bolts may be made of any material and length, but not be of· such design as to cause unreasonable damage to the target boss. They shall be plainly crested for easy scoring. Bolt length should not be less than 12in.

10   Spotting aids: binoculars or a spotting scope may be used at any time to locate hits. Spotting scopes must be set up in the tackle area. This rule is for target shoots only, not field shoots.

11   Sights: telescopic or magnifying sights shall not be permitted.

12   Bow weight: in flight shooting or other events where the bow weight is a governing factor in the competition, the various classifications set up shall be figured in direct proportion to the longbow for that class at 27in draw, using the in/lb method to determine the class into which the bow may fall.

Standard classifications for flight bows are:

For ladies: 35lb; 50lb; and unlimited.

For men: 50lb; 65lb; 80lb; and unlimited.

For example a ladies' bow weighing 50lb at 16in draw (a common draw for a crossbow) would fall in the 35lb class; $16 \times 50 = 800$in/lb, the upper limit for the class being 945in/lb ($27 \times 35 = 945$).

Crossbow Flight Conversion Table

35lb class	Upper limit 945in/lb
50lb class	Upper limit 1,350in/lb
65lb class	Upper limit 1,755in/lb
80lb class	Upper limit 2,160in/lb

Unlimited class: any bow weighing over 2,160in/lb.

13   Target bosses shall be of woven or compressed straw or grass of the greatest degree of firmness obtainable. Rectangular bales of straw are not considered suitable for crossbows.

14 Safety: Crossbowmen will keep their weapons when drawn, whether loaded or not, pointed in the direction of the target. All safety rules laid down by the EFAA for longbow archers also pertain to crossbowmen.

15 Infraction of rules: The Crossbow Field Captain may at his discretion penalise or even bar from further competition a shooter who exhibits carelessness in handling his weapon, or whose weapon he considers to be dangerous to other shooters or spectators.

16 Age limit: no crossbowmen under the age of sixteen years may shoot at a National Championship meeting unless in adult care.

17 Championship rounds shall consist of a double British Crossbow Round, 5doz at 60yd, 5doz at 50yd, 5doz at 40yd. The target shall be as stated in Rule 2.

18 The *maximum* draw weight per length of draw, expressed in in/lb for alloy (metal) and composite (wood and fibreglass) prods.

(*a*) Alloy prods: 1,600in/lb at 16in draw length;

(*b*) Composite prods: 1,280in/lb at 12in draw length.

To determine the in/lb draw weight multiply the draw weight of your prod by the draw length, ie:

$$80lb \times 16in = 1,280in/lb$$
$$85lb \times 15in = 1,275in/lb$$

The draw length in all cases to be measured from the back of the prod, the part of the prod nearest to the front end of the stock, to the string groove in the latch.

CLASSIFICATION (TARGET SHOOTS)

Master Arbalist To gain the title of Master Arbalist a member must shoot three British Crossbow Rounds of 650 during any period of two consecutive years. The title to be held for a period of two calendar years. If a crossbowman fails to complete the qualification inside one year he or she may carry over any scores made during that year into the following year, but no further.

First-Class Arbalist   Three British Crossbow Rounds of 550 must be shot during the calendar year, one round to be shot at an open meeting recognised by the BCS.

Arbalist   Three*British Crossbow Rounds of 450 must be shot during the calendar year, one round at an open meeting recognised by the BCS. All scores to be submitted to Hon Secretary, BCS or Area Secretary.

CLASSIFICATION (FIELD SHOOTS)

Men

500 and over	Grand Field Master Arbalist
400 to 499	Field Master Arbalist
300 to 399	Field Expert Arbalist
0 to 299	Field Arbalist

Ladies and Juniors (Juniors are under sixteen years of age)

400 and over	Grand Field Master Arbalist
325 to 399	Field Master Arbalist
250 to 324	Field Expert Arbalist
0 to 249	Field Arbalist

The FITA Rules of Field Shooting

The current rules, taken from the official rule book, are as follows:

Art 800: Terms

Unit a 14-target course including all official shots

Round two such units or twice around one

Double Round two complete rounds

Post shooting position

Face target face

Butt any object against which a face is placed

Shot this term in connection with the post number, eg '4th shot' shall be used in referring to the different shots on any course

Spot aiming centre

Field Round

Art 801: Faces

Four face sizes shall be used:

  (*a*) A 60cm diam face, a 30cm centre ring and a 10cm spot;

  (*b*) A 45cm diam face, a 22·5cm centre ring and a 7·5cm spot;

  (*c*) A 30cm diam face, a 15cm centre ring and a 5cm spot;

  (*d*) A 15cm diam face, a 7·5cm centre ring and a 2·5cm spot.

The outside ring shall be black, the centre ring white. The spot shall be black.

Animal targets bearing these official round faces may also be used. In this case the faces need not be painted, only outlined, but the spot must be of a contrasting colour, plainly visible. If the faces are only outlined, the line shall be inside the scoring area.

Art 802

All butts must be so placed that the full face is exposed to the shooter.

Art 803

A standard field round unit shall consist of the following fourteen shots:

15, 20, 25 and 30m at a 30cm diam face (four arrows at each distance);

35, 40 and 45m at a 45cm diam face (four arrows at each distance);

50, 55 and 60m at a 60cm diam face (four arrows at each distance).

And the following four position shots—each arrow to be shot from a different position or at a different target:

35m at a 45cm diam face, all from the same distance (the fan shot);

30, 35, 40 and 45m at a 45cm diam face;

45, 55, 65 and 75m at a 60cm diam face;

6, 8, 10 and 12m at a 15cm diam face.

Art 804

A 5 per cent variation in distance is permitted where necessary because of terrain. All shortages, however, must be made up on another target in the same unit. In laying out the course any order may be used as the official shooting order on any four position shot. All fourteen shots shall be mixed to give maximum of variety.

Art 805

Each archer shall shoot four arrows at each of the fourteen target layouts in a unit. In ten cases this shall mean shooting the four arrows from a single post at a single face. In the other four

114

cases it may mean either shooting one arrow from each of four posts at a single face, or it may mean shooting all four arrows from a single post but at four separate faces.

The Hunter's Round
Art 806: Faces
Four face sizes shall be used as in the field round. The faces shall be either all black with a white spot and with the ringing invisible from the post, or they can be animal targets with the spot of a contrasting colour. The centre ring shall be inside the animal figure and the ringing invisible from the post (this is not a must for the 15cm diam faces).
Art 807
All butts must be so placed that the full face is exposed to the shooter.
Art 808
A standard hunter's round unit shall consist of the following fourteen shots:

> 5–15m at a 15cm diam face. There shall be two such targets with a total distance of 50m for six arrows;
> 10–30m at a 30cm diam face. There shall be four such targets with a total distance of 240m for twelve arrows;
> 20–40m at a 45cm diam face. There shall be five such targets with a total distance of 450m for fifteen arrows;
> 30–50m at a 60cm diam face. There shall be three such targets with a total distance of 360m for nine arrows.

The grand total length of a unit shall be 1,100m for forty-two arrows. The distances shall be exact.
Art 809
Each archer shall shoot three arrows at each of the fourteen target layouts in a unit and each arrow shall be shot from a different post.

Shooting Rules
Art 810

Any kind of bow (except a crossbow) and any kind of arrow, except broadheads or arrows that would unreasonably injure a target face, may be used in any event unless otherwise stated.
Art 811

A Field Captain shall be appointed and it shall be his duties to:

(a)   See that a target captain and two scorers are appointed for each group.

(b)   Designate the order in which groups are to shoot or assign the posts, from which each group is to start, depending on what system is used.

(c)   Be the final authority in settling any disputes that may arise over rules or conduct of the tournament.

Art 812

The duty of the Target Captain shall be to order the shooting at his target and to settle all local questions. His decision on arrow values shall be final. Other decisions may be appealed to the Field Captain. It is also his duty to report any archer in his group violating the rules.
Art 813

The scorers shall keep an account of every arrow that hits the target and at each target compare the scores.
Art 814

Archers shall shoot in groups of not less than three or more than five, four shall be the preferred number.
Art 815

Arrows must remain untouched in the face until withdrawn by the Target Captain or his deputy in the presence of the scorers.
Art 816

The archers in a group shall be divided into A, B, C, D and E shots and the shooting shall take place in rotating order. A shoots first followed by B and so on. At the next target B shoots first and A last. Wherever possible two archers shall shoot at the same time, one from each side of the post. If there are three in a group A and B shoot together and C alone; at the next target B and C start and A shoots alone. The same system shall be used if the group consists of five archers.

Archers shall stand with both feet back of the shooting line and no one shall approach the target until all have finished shooting. When shooting at the 15cm diam face scoring shall be allowed after each archer has shot his arrows. When shooting at the 30cm diam face scoring shall be allowed after two archers have shot their arrows. The shooting line is an imagined line, parallel to the target.

Art 817

One group shall not hold up the following groups while looking for lost arrows. Enough arrows shall be carried so that each archer may continue shooting and return later to find missing arrows.

Art 818

An archer who has to stop shooting because of a broken string or similar cause shall complete his shooting before the group leaves the shot. This means that spare strings shall be carried along. A broken bow may be replaced by a borrowed bow.

Scoring

Art 819

The scoring is five points for the centre ring including spot and three points for the outer ring.

Art 820

The status of arrows shall be determined before drawing any arrows from the face. An arrow shall not be touched until after being recorded. The value of an arrow shall be determined by the arrow-shaft's situation in the face, not by the hole it may have torn in the face.

Art 821

The Target Captain shall be the final judge of all disputed arrows.

Art 822

An arrow touching a ring shall be scored as being inside the

117

scoring field. For that reason the arrow must touch the line so that no colour of the outside field can be seen between the arrow-shaft and the line.

The same is true for the inner line between the two circles.

Art 823

Skids or glances into the target shall not be counted.

Art 824

Arrows passing through the face, but still in the butt, may be pushed back and scored as a hit in the circle through which they went. This does not mean that they may be withdrawn and then stuck back through the target. Telescoping arrows shall have the same value.

Art 825

Witnessed bounces or arrows passing through the face may be scored as three points.

Art 826

No group of less than three shall turn in an official score.

Art 827

No archer may practise on any shot of the tournament course, nor shall there be any practice targets supplied or put up by the archers themselves on or close to the tournament area.

Art 828

In case of a tie in the total score the order of the archers shall be determined by:

(*a*)   The greatest number of hit targets.

(*b*)   The greatest number of scoring arrows (hits).

(*c*)   If there is still a draw the order shall be determined by shooting off on a sufficient number of targets starting with shot No 1.

General

Art 829

Faces shall not be placed over any larger target, nor shall there be any marks on the butt or foreground that could be used as points of aim.

118

Art 830
All posts shall be numbered but the distances may not be given.
Art 831
Women may compete against men, but men may not compete in women's events.
Art 832
Instinctive and free-style archers shall shoot in separate classes. Archers shooting in instinctive class must use bow free from any sights, marks or blemishes that could be used in aiming. This applies to the string also (see Art 837).

In free-style class any type of sight may be used, except one calibrated for the course.
Art 833
In tournaments where no distinction is made between the two styles of shooting, the only sight that shall be allowed is a single narrow stationary mark not exceeding 3mm in width or a single fixed sight of similar dimension.
Art 834
At no time shall any device be allowed that would by any manner be of aid in estimating the distance of any shot. The use of field glasses or binoculars is prohibited. Nor may the archer refer to any memoranda of any kind that could in any manner be a means of improving his or her score.
Art 835
The use of a mechanical release shall be illegal. Interpretation of mechanical release shall be a device comprising a plurality of interactive parts, whether such are individual pieces or spring conjoined parts, capable of co-operatively acting to effect bow-string release by a separate motion of at least one such part relative to another such part.
Art 836
It shall be permissible to use two or more posts at any or all of one position shots providing, however, that the posts are equidistant from the target.

Art 837
Instinctive archers must use bows free from any sights, marks or blemishes which could be used for aiming. The inside of the upper limb shall be completely free from all protuberances, marks, blemishes, trade marks, etc. The ends or edges of laminated pieces shall not be considered provided that the bow is not specially constructed to provide for a graduated system. The bowstring shall be of one colour. The serving may be a different colour from that of the bowstring provided the serving is one colour. There shall be no hanging threads. There shall not be more than one nocking point.

Art 838
A dropped arrow or a failure shot where the arrow falls to the ground within reach of the archer's bow, when he or she is standing at the post, may be fetched by the archer and shall not be considered as having been shot.

Art 839
No arrow under any circumstances can be reshot.

Art 840
A Technical Committee, with the Field Captain as chairman, shall be elected before the start of the tournament. This committee shall control the archers' equipment before the tournament is started and shall serve as a jury to deal with possible protests against individuals or arrangements. Such protests must be delivered in writing to the Technical Committee at the latest an hour after the completion of the shooting and under all circumstances before the distribution of prizes.

The NAA Championships: Official Tournament Rules

8.0   Shooting, scoring and conduct of participants.

8.3   There shall be at least three uninterrupted practice ends, at the longest distance, followed without interruption by the beginning of scoring for the round.

8.4   There shall be no practice permitted after a postponement or delay, unless such postponement or delay exceeds 30 minutes. In such cases the amount of practice shall be according to the following schedule:

1   30- to 60-minute delay: one practice end;
2   60 minutes or more delay unless interrupted by a scheduled lunch period or nightfall: two practice ends.

8.7   If an archer shoots less than six arrows in one end, he may shoot the remaining arrows if the omission is discovered before the end is officially completed; otherwise, they shall score as misses.

8.8   If an archer shoots more than six arrows in one end, only the lowest six shall score.

8.13   If an arrow in a target touches two colours, breaking the inside edge of the black scoring line, the higher colour shall count. Doubtful arrows must be determined for each end and before the arrows or target face have been touched; otherwise, the lower value must be taken.

8.14 An arrow that has passed through the scoring face so that it is not visible from the front shall count seven at 60yd, or less, and five for ranges beyond 60yd. Arrows passing completely through the target, if witnessed, shall score in the same manner.

8.15 An arrow which rebounds from the scoring face, if witnessed, shall score the same as a pass through.

8.16 Hits on the wrong target shall score as misses.

8.23 Any archer may retire from the shooting line to avoid proximity to a tackle or a shooting practice that he considers unsafe, and may resume shooting when safe conditions prevail.

8.26 The scores shall be resolved in favour of the archer shooting the highest score at the longest distance; then next longest distance, in descending order. If still tied through all distances, then ties shall be resolved in favour of the archer with the greatest number of Golds, Reds, Blues, then Blacks. If still tied the tie shall be resolved in favour of the archer with the greatest number of perfect ends. If still tied it shall be so recorded.

8.27 Coaching an archer on the shooting line by means of inaudible and inconspicuous signs or symbols is permitted, provided that such coaching is not distracting to other contestants. If a contestant on the same target, or adjacent target, complains that such activity is personally distracting, such coaching must be terminated immediately. Audible coaching of archers on the shooting line is not permitted.

1.8 Bow racks, tackle, boxes or other objects which protrude above the ground shall not be allowed within 6ft of the shooting line.

Crossbow Tournament Rules, Revised and Corrected

13.1   Crossbowmen do not compete with longbowmen. They compete with and against each other for awards within their own division.

13.2   Rules are the same as for longbowmen except where in conflict with the rules given in this section.

13.3   The Crossbow Field Captain is specifically appointed to supervise the crossbowmen. His duties and authority correspond to that of the Field Captain for the longbowmen, his decision being final unless appealed to the Board.

13.4   The Crossbows and parts may be made of any safe material. The "traditional" type crossbow shall be used, namely, the bow shall be fitted to a stock in a horizontal position.

13.5   Bow Weight: In flight shooting, or in other events where the weight of the bow is a governing factor in the competition, the various classifications set up shall be figured in direct proportion to the longbow for that class at twenty-seven inches draw, using the inch-pound method to determine the class in which the bow may fall. For Target shooting, it is recommended that the bow be limited to 80 pounds for outdoor shooting and 50 pounds for indoor shooting.

13.6 Drawing: Crossbows shall be drawn by hand. No mechanical aids shall be permitted for spanning the bow, however, the Field Captain may permit a physically incapacitated contestant the use of a mechanical spanning aid in order to compete. Foot stirrups attached to the stock or foot plates on the ground will be allowed.

13.7 Arrows: (or Bolts) may be made of any material, but must not be of such design that they will unreasonably damage the target face or bast. They should be plainly marked for ease in scoring.

13.8 Safety: Crossbowmen will keep their weapons when drawn, whether loaded or not, pointed in the direction of the target. The Crossbow Field Captain may, at his discretion, reprimand or even bar from further competition a crossbow he considers dangerous to other shooters or spectators. All safety rules specified for longbowmen also pertain to crossbowmen.

13.9 Shooting: Crossbowmen stand to shoot and shall shoot "offhand." No rest or straps of any description shall be permitted. The Field Captain may permit a physically incapacitated contestant to shoot while seated.

13.10 Sights: Magnifying sights shall not be permitted. Level bubbles, prismatic sights and other optical non-magnifying sights are allowed.

13.11 Spotting Aids: Binoculars or spotting scopes may be used at any time to locate hits. Spotting scopes may be left on the shooting line at the discretion of the Field Captain.

13.12 Infractions of Rules: The Crossbow Field Captain shall have the responsibility and authority to interpret and to decide questions of rules in accordance with regulations and customs.

13.13 Target Backstops: (or Basts) shall be the same as those used by the longbowmen.

13.14 Targets: Target faces for the crossbow championship round shall be the standard 80 cm. F.I.T.A. target face. Crossbow archers use the same size target as do longbowmen for Clout, F.I.T.A. I & II Rounds. For crossbow events which have no counterpart in the Longbow Division, such as the King's and Queen's Rounds, the appropriate target faces shall be used.

13.15 Rounds: The National Championship for both Gentlemen and Ladies shall be determined by the highest total scores shot, by each sex, in the Quadruple International Crossbow Round. The tournament officials may, at their discretion, add such other events as it considers desirable, such as Clout, King's and Queen's Rounds, novelty rounds, etc., but the scores made in such events shall not count toward determining the championship.

13.16 International Crossbow Round:

> 30 Arrows at 65 M (71.1 yds.)
> 30 Arrows at 50 M (54.7 yds.)
> 30 Arrows at 35 M (38.3 yds.)

An optional six practice arrows will be permitted prior to official scoring at each distance. Perfect Score – 900.

13.17 Awards:

Gentlemen: First, second, third place NAA medals for permanent possession.

Ladies: First, second, third place NAA medals for permanent possession.

The Fred Isles Cup: Gentleman's National Crossbow Champion.

The H. L. Bailey Trophy: Lady's National Crossbow Champion.

The Karl Traudt Award: The high single International Crossbow Round.

The Anderson Award: The Crossbow Clout Champion.

The Stevens Dagger: The King's Round Champion.

The Queen's Scepter: The Queen's Round Champion.

13.18 Heraldry: In addition to the foregoing awards, The National Crossbowmen of the United States have rules governing the decoration of pennons or gonfalons which may be displayed. These rules may be obtained from The National Crossbowmen thru the Secretary-Treasurer of The National Crossbowmen.

INSERT
FUTURE RULES
AND
REGULATIONS
HERE

All-time US Target Crossbow Records

Women

American Round 60cm. Target
900 Possible. 60, 50, 40 yards

Single American	787	Carol Pelosi	1974
Quadruple American	3034	Carol Pelosi	1975

Metric 900 Round 60cm. Target
900 Possible. 60, 50, 40 meters

Single Metric	811	Carol Pelosi	1981

International Crossbow Round
80cm. Target
900 Possible. 65, 50, 35 meters

Single International	840	Carol Pelosi	1978
Quadruple International	3309	Carol Pelosi	1978

Clout Shoot
324 Possible. 180 yards

	292	Margaret Breneman	1958

Queens Round
60 Possible. 35 meters

	56	Carol Pelosi	1978

Fita I (Indoor) 40cm. Target
600 Possible. 18 meters

	600	Carol Pelosi	1981

Fita II (Indoor) 60cm. Target
600 Possible. 25 meters

	593	Carol Pelosi	1979

Fita I & II (Indoor)
1200 Possible. Combined   1192   Carol Pelosi   1981

Men

American Round 60cm. Target
900 Possible. 60, 50, 40 yards
Single American   825   Rolfe Smith   1978
Double American   1626   Rolfe Smith   1978
Quadruple American   3235   Rolfe Smith   1978

Metric 900 Round 60cm. Target
900 Possible. 60, 50, 40 meters
Single Metric   833   Alan Kaufhold   1982
Double Metric   1582   Rolfe Smith   1981

International Crossbow Round
80cm. Target
900 Possible. 65, 50, 35 meters
Single International   866   Ervin Myers   1981
Quadruple International   3415   Ervin Myers   1981

Clout Shoot
324 Possible. 180 yards   307   Col. F. E. Pierce   1956

Kings Round
60 Possible. 35 meters   57   Alan Kaufhold   1981

Fita I (Indoor) 40cm. Target
600 Possible. 18 meters   599   Ervin Myers   1982

Fita II (Indoor) 60cm. Target
600 Possible. 25 meters   598   Charles Sacco   1980

Fita I & II (Indoor)
1200 Possible. Combined   1194   Charles Sacco   1978

Safety-first Rules

For Your Equipment

1 Never pull the trigger of a cocked crossbow without a bolt in the breech.
2 If your equipment gets wet, dry it thoroughly and oil it as soon as possible.
3 Never leave your equipment where children could handle it unsupervised.
4 Never draw the string of a crossbow with one hand only. It will strain one limb and pull the string out of line.
5 Never shoot with a string that is badly frayed or has threads broken.

For Yourself and Others

1 Never point a loaded crossbow in the direction of anyone even in fun.
2 When shooting in competition never place a bolt in the breach until standing on the shooting line and pointing the crossbow in the direction of the target.
3 Never shoot straight up into the air.
4 Never shoot a bolt so that you cannot see where it may fall (eg over trees, hills or buildings). There may be someone in the way unseen by you.
5 Always make sure no one is behind or near the target when you are shooting.
6 If you *must* shoot with a metal prod, always use some method of preventing the pieces flying about and injuring yourself or others should it shatter.

Glossary of Terms

American round thirty bolts at 60yd, 50yd and 40yd

Arbalest crossbow

Arrowsmith one who fashions metal arrow-heads

Backing any material suitable for backing a bow

Belly the surface of a bow nearest the archer in shooting

Black the target ring of that colour, or a hit in it; value three

Blue the target ring of that colour, or a hit in it; value five

Bolt the missile (or arrow) of a crossbow

Bolt Channel see *Groove*

Boss the straw back of a target made by bending and sewing the straw into a compact circular mat

Bowyer a bow maker

Brace to string or bend a bow

Broadhead the hunting head of a bolt; formerly used in warfare

Butt a mound upon which a shooting mark (the butt-mark, a small paper disc) was pinned. Hence butt-arrow, butt-shaft, butt-shooting, etc

Butt (of a crossbow) the rear end that is held on or against the shoulder

Cast the speed of a bow. The distance a bow will shoot

Catch see *Latch*

Centre shot bow or prod which is cut away in centre to allow the bolt to pass more easily

Clout a small white target with a black centre used in long-distance shooting; originally the white cloth used as a target

Composite bow   one built up of wood in conjunction with other materials, usually fibreglass. Other materials used are rattan, fibrous barks, whalebone, horn and sinew

Cocking   getting the string on to the catch

Crest   the archer's distinctive bolt decoration; the painted bands on a bolt

Draw   the distance a given bow is properly pulled, or the effort (expressed in pounds or kilogrammes) required to draw it (the draw weight)

End   in formal shooting, the number of bolts shot consecutively or otherwise by each archer before the score is taken

Face   of a bow (*qv*). Of a target, the painted scoring surface

Feather   a whole feather or one of the sections on a bolt

Field Captain   the officer in charge of a tournament or formal shoot

FITA round   men: thirty-six bolts at 90m, 70m, 50m, and 30m, on ten zone targets; ladies: 70m, 60m, 50m, and 30m

Fletch   to prepare and apply the feathers to a bolt

Fletcher   one who makes arrows or feathers them

Fletching   the feathers on a bolt whether of natural (turkey, goose, etc) or of plastic material

Flight   how or how far a bolt flies (many bolts flying together), flight as a form of contest (to shoot for great distance) hence flight shooter, flight shooting, flight shot

Flight bow   a strong or fast-casting bow capable of great distance

Flirt   a wobble or deviation in the flight of a bolt

Fish arrow   one with a detachable harpoon-shaped head on a line

Footed bolt   one with hardwood spliced on front of shaft

Former   shaped wooden board on which the prod is glued up until the glue is set

Gold   the centre of the regulation target, or a hit in it; value nine

Groove   channel in which bolt runs

Hunting head   special point on a bolt used for killing game

Hypodart or hypodermic   dart carrying a tranquillising drug

Judge   an official at a tournament who can be appealed to in questions of scoring

Lady Paramount   lady who presides over a tournament and presents prizes

Latch   hook that holds the string at full draw

Limb   the right or left half of a bow

Longbow   generally any bow (not a crossbow) of traditional English shape whose mid-limb depth from back to belly is almost as great as its width at the same point, and whose width is nowhere greater than at the grip

Loose or loosing   the act of loosing the string and bolt simultaneously

Main String   shooting string

Overdrawn   bow or bolt drawn too far

Peep-sight   a device, usually on the stock, by which the gold is sighted directly. In particular a pin-sight set in a ring

Petticoat   the narrow painted circle that bounds the white of a regulation target and marks the limit of the scoring area (it has no value) or a hit in the straw on margin of target

Pile   the bolt tip or point, especially one that is cylindrical or conical in shape (in contrast to broad-heads or barbed-heads which are flat)

Point-blank shooting   shooting at the distance at which no allowance needs to be made for the effect of gravity on the bolt, the distance at which the bolt flies straight to the mark

Popinjay (pepingoe)   a wooden figure (bird supposedly) set upon a high pole as an archery mark

Prince's colours   the five rings on the target instituted by George IV when Prince of Wales

Prod   the bow part of a crossbow

Quarrell   special bolt for piercing plate armour

Quiver   a bag or case for carrying bolts usually of leather and worn on the person

Range   the shooting-field; one of the distances of a round; the greatest distance of which a given bow is capable

Recurve   shape of prod where limbs curve back and then forward to increase leverage

Red   the target ring of that colour or a hit in it; value seven

Reflexed bow   a bow so constructed that the limbs assume a concave or angular relation when it is unstrung

Round   a definite number of shots at definite distances, constituting a form of competition

Rovers or roving   a form of archery contest in which the archer or archers progress from mark to mark; or the mark shot at in this fashion. Hence roving bolt, roving bow, rover pile, etc.

Score   20yd (eg ten score); number of points gained

Secondary string   an aid in bending the bow to fit the main string

Self   of a bow or bolt, consisting essentially of one piece of wood (by itself); the bolt may be knocked but not footed

Serving-jig   small spool of thread on a fitting that revolves round the string to serve or bind it

Shaft   of a bolt, the wooden part or the bolt itself; of a feather, a quill

Shaftment (or shaftmond)   the part of a shaft covered by the feathers

Sight   see *Peep-sight*. To sight; to aim

Stance   see *Standing*

Stand   the tripod on which the target hangs

Standing   the correct footing and attitude assumed by crossbowmen before beginning to shoot

Stave   the piece of wood from which the bow is made

String   the bowstring. To string: to brace the bow

Stock   hand-held part of crossbow

Tackle   archery equipment, in the same sense as fishing tackle

Tassel   a tassel of coloured yarn worn at the archer's belt for cleaning arrows

Tiller   essentially a board with a rest at one end for the handle of a bow, and a series of notches for the string along its side. It is used for holding the bow bent while its shape is studied. To tiller: to bring a bow to balance and check its curvature

Target face   canvas or paper scoring area

Trigger   part of mechanism that releases catch

Vane   the section of feather ready to affix or already affixed to the bolt; the soft, blade-like part of the feather to either side of the quill (also called Web)

Wand   a stick thrust into the ground for a mark

Web   see *Vane*

Weight   of a bow, its drawing weight; the measure of force expressed in pounds or kilogrammes required to draw the bow and cock the string. Of a bolt, its actual weight expressed in grains, grammes, or shillings and sixpences

White   the outermost scoring circle of the target, or a hit in it; value one

York Round   seventy-two bolts at 100yd, forty-eight at 80yd and twenty-four at 60yd

Useful Addresses

Associations

The National Archery
Assocation
1750 E. Boulder Street
Colorado Springs, CO 80909

The National Crossbowmen
of the USA
Longwood Gardens
Kennett Square, PA 19348

Magazines

The British Archer
68 The Dale
Widley, Portsmouth
P07 5DE, UK

The Crossbow Chit Chat—
The National Crossbowmen
of the USA
c/o National Archery Association
1750 E. Boulder Street
Colorado Springs, CO 80909

*The Journal of the Society of
Archer Antiquaries*
71 St. John's Road
Swalecliffe, Whitsatable
Kent, UK

Suppliers

Dave Benedict Crossbows
Box 343
Chatsworth, CA 91311

Full Adjust Archery Products
915 North Ann Street
Lancaster, PA 17602

Martin Crossbows
Rt. #5 Box 65
Huntsville, AK 72740

136

Index